PARIS HILTON

LIFE ON THE EDGE

PARIS HILTON

LIFE ON THE EDGE

THE BIOGRAPHY

CHAS NEWKEY-BURDEN

JOHN BLAKE

Chas Newkey-Burden is the author of a number of books including *Great Email Disasters* and *The Reduced History Of Britain*. A prolific journalist, he has interviewed a galaxy of stars including David Beckham, Dennis Bergkamp, Steve Coogan, Rachel Stevens, Jenna Jameson, Ant and Dec and McFly for a host of magazines including *Attitude*, *Loaded* and *The Big Issue*. He is currently co-writing a book with Julie Burchill.

This book is dedicated to Pen.

Published by John Blake Publishing Ltd,
3 Bramber Court, 2 Bramber Road,
London W14 9PB, UK

www.blake.co.uk

First published in paperback in 2007

ISBN: 978-1-84454-457-8

British Library Cataloguing-in-Publication Data:
A catalogue record for this book is available from the British Library.

Design by www.envydesign.co.uk

Printed in Great Britain by William Clowes Ltd, Beccles, Suffolk.

1 3 5 7 9 10 8 6 4 2

Papers used by John Blake Publishing are natural, recyclable products made from wood
grown in sustainable forests. The manufacturing processes conform to the environmental
regulations of the country of origin.

Every effort has been made to contact relevant copyright holders. Any omission is
inadvertent; we would be grateful if the appropriate people could contact us.

CONTENTS

ACKNOWLEDGEMENTS

Special thanks to Chris Morris, Julie Burchill, Lucian Randall and Stuart Robertson.

I'd also like to sincerely thank the following for their help, encouragement and support either with this book specifically or just generally down the years: Mum, Dad, Tristan, Pen, Rose, May and Verity, Judy Kerr, Yaara Shalom, Jamie Hakim, Matt Ford, Matthew Collin, Andrew Davies, Will Jessop, Clare Christian, Clare Webber, Paul Carr, Scott Pack, Adam Higginbotham, Matt Parselle, Michelle Olley, Richard Jones, Justyn Barnes, Joe Parry, John Perry, Chas Chandler, Rob Kemp, John Blake, Roland Hall, Martin Corteel, Trevor Davies, Eleanor Levy, Robert Caskie, Mark Simpson, Katie Glass, Nigel Horne, Simon Hogg, Michelle Signore, Oliver Marre, Diana Colbert, Bill Borrows, Andrew Shields, Sam Pilger, Henry Winter and everyone I've forgotten.

INTRODUCTION

'Some girls always get what they wanna wanna,' goes the famous pop song, and although it was sung by a different glamorous blonde celebrity – former S Club 7 member Rachel Stevens – the words could so easily have been written for Paris Hilton. This 'It' girl has got it all: a super-wealthy family, dazzling good looks and a figure to die for. She has strutted down the catwalk at top fashion shows across the world, and designed purses, a jewellery line and a range of watches. Her inheritance, when it comes, looks set to be around £20 million – although it must be stated that since she turned 18, Paris has earned every penny of her money herself.

Her album *Paris* and autobiography *Confessions Of An Heiress* were eagerly snapped off the shelves by her legion of fans. Her acting career goes from strength to strength: from bit-part roles playing herself to leading roles in major movies like *House Of Wax* and *The Hottie And The Nottie*, she's seen off the critics who sniggered behind their popcorn at the very thought of an It girl making it big on the big screen. After her charismatic and hilarious performance on reality television show *The Simple Life*, her cinematic success should really have come as no surprise at all. She has also raised many thousands of pounds for a range of charities including Toys For Tots, a group that gives gifts to poor children and the Room To Grow charity, which benefits babies born into poverty. She is a lifelong animal-lover and has raised awareness of animal welfare issues for many years.

Then there are the men who have been part of her incredible story. From actor Leonardo DiCaprio to pop star Nick Carter and model Jason Shaw, she has enjoyed a procession of beautiful young men falling at her shapely, extravagantly clad feet. Even when those relationships have subsequently ended, rarely has Paris seemed at all needy or vengeful in the aftermath. Rather than running to the press to slag off her former love, she has instead sauntered off to write the next chapter of her own incredible story.

At the risk of committing the understatement of the millennium, it is fair to say that the media has for a long time been interested in documenting Paris's story, as was seen in the ravenous feeding frenzy that greeted her jailing in 2007. On one of the tracks on her album, Paris jokes that she'll give us something to write about. Never was a truer word sung: for many years she has shown an exceptional knack for getting photographers' cameras to snap and journalists' keyboards to tap. If you want to get something mentioned in the press, and PR guru Max Clifford won't take your call, you could do a lot worse than ask Paris for a bit of advice. In comparison, she makes our own Jordan look like a shy, reclusive hermit. Indeed, Paris could probably teach David and Victoria Beckham a thing or two about self-promotion.

She has even trademarked her own catchphrase: 'That's hot'. She used this phrase throughout *The Simple Life* series and it really caught on with fans across the world. When asked how she felt about her phrase entering the lexicon of so many of her fans, her reply was an inevitable: 'That's hot'. She then revealed, 'I trademarked the phrase about seven months ago. I've been saying it forever. I want to put it on T-shirts and stuff like that.'

So, is Paris the girl who's got it all? If she is, then in truth part of 'it all' also includes things that nobody would want. The spotlight might look a lot of fun from the outside but when you're in the centre of the media glare, life can be very painful and difficult at times. When videos of her in bed with her boyfriend were leaked it must have become almost unbearable for a while. Likewise, when an LA court sentenced her to 45 days in jail for driving offences, her shock and pain can only have been multiplied by the fact that a crowd of journalists filled the court and an even more huge and hungry mob were waiting outside to snap her as she left the building in a state of shock. Everyone messes up their lives at some point, but most of us are lucky enough not to have the media spotlight on us when we take a wrong step.

Paris has said that she feels the media often uses her as a punch-bag and admits that wherever she goes, she hears the shutters of the paparazzi cameras – whether they are there or not. However, they invariably are there, right in front of her, snapping away. 'No matter what I'm doing, they're there,' she sighs. 'It's so annoying. Everywhere in LA, even if I do sometimes get away from them, everywhere I go they have contacts who'll call them: "Paris is here." Then another guy comes. Then there's 30 of them. You can't even get your mail or put the trash out or do anything – they're gonna take a picture of you.' The snappers adore Paris; as one of their number commented: 'Paris Hilton is a phenomenon. She's sexy, smart, gracious and kind, and there's no one like her in the past and I doubt there will be another one like her in the future. She's always giving us variations on the red carpet, posing this way and that, and this is what a photographer wants: variety you know, moving around. Because that's what life is about – movement.'

Paris was once asked if there has ever been a time when she has needed the press. 'No. I can understand, going to a press event, say a movie premiere for something I'm in. Then it's OK; you're on the press line, that's where they're supposed to be. But not outside your house every single day, like a stalker. I don't want them following me to my celebrity friends' houses – I don't want them knowing where they live. So I always have to get away and when I'm doing that, then I drive really fast…' It's hard not to draw parallels with another beautiful young blonde woman who the media became obsessed with. It is to be hoped that Paris's story does not end in a similar tragedy.

Then there is the extreme envy that Paris seems to provoke in some sour observers. Rich people often attract jealousy, so do successful people and so do good-looking people. Paris is all three of those things, so she seems destined for a lifetime of nasty snaps from envious people who have put her in a no-win situation. If she does nothing, they sneer and call her spoiled lazy girl. However, when she makes something of herself through business ventures, television shows and films, they attack her for being greedy and ask why someone who is set to inherit so much money should try and earn more. How dare she? By the same token, whenever she does something that even the bitterest heart would have to accept is clever, successful and positive, they have another retort lined up: nothing she does is down to her, it's the people around her who pull all the strings in her life so they are the clever ones, not her. However, when something she does is silly or unsuccessful, the same critics quickly forget about 'the people around her' and instead heap all the responsibility on to Paris – I told you she was dumb.

Her critics come in all shapes and sizes. Broadcaster Stephen Fry once said that to be Paris Hilton, you need 'a startling vanity, an enormous lack of self-knowledge and a huge amount of greed and desire.' Partridge Family star,

David Cassidy, once hissed, 'What does she do? Well, she doesn't really do anything except go to nightclubs.' Meanwhile, pop singer, Pink, made thinly veiled digs at Paris and other 'porno paparazzi girls' in her song *Stupid Girls*. These sorts of digs are so easy to make – as is the mantra repeated by so many about Paris: that she is famous for being famous. This is a hollow and monotonous accusation. However, those that level this accusation at her invariably do so as if they are the only person who has ever thought of the line. Such are the delusions of intellect of many of Paris's detractors.

A naturally positive and generously spirited person, Paris finds envy and the abuse it leads to particularly hurtful. 'It's not my fault that I was born with this,' she pleads. 'I thank God and I'm lucky, and I help people and I give money away, and I do a lot of things for people. I realise I'm lucky – and people shouldn't hate me for that. They should hate me if I'm a bad person and mean to people. But I'm so sweet. I'm too nice.' This is indeed a sweet defence but perhaps too sweet.

A more direct retort to the critics came from Paris's younger sister Nicky: 'I just want to say to these writers I'm 21 years old, I run two multi-million-dollar companies, I work my ass off,' she snapped. 'Like, what were you doing that was so f*cking important at my age? I feel very accomplished for my age. And Paris – I mean, the movies, the fragrance, the book, the album... and people just love to take everything away from us. I don't know why. Maybe they feel it was just handed to us. Yeah, we were born with a famous last name. I get that. But just look at how we took it to another level.'

Another level? Absolutely! Paris was estimated by *Forbes* magazine to have made £4 million in 2004 from promoting herself, and the magazine ranked her as the 55th most powerful celebrity in the USA, above Bill Clinton at number 56. Other sources claim she earned four times more than that. 'There's nobody who can generate as much as I can for events,' she insists, and the American public seem to agree. 'They did a poll in the States asking people who they'd most like to see at a party – and it was me.' She regularly tops The Lycos 50, a list of the most popular user searches for the previous week on the Internet group. When George Bush gave his much-vaunted blockbuster interview to Diane Sawyer on ABC News' *PrimeTime Live* show just hours after Saddam Hussein was captured in Iraq, more Americans chose to watch Paris and Nicole Richie playing in a kissing booth at a fête on *The Simple Life*. Some 11.9 million viewers chose Paris, while just 11 million tuned in to listen to Bush, which led to a *Washington Post* headline that read: 'Paris Outdraws The Prez!' The accompanying story suggested that 'the Democrats should run Paris Hilton for president.' She drew 22 per cent of 18- to 34-year-olds who were watching, while only seven per cent of them were watching Sawyer lob questions at the president. On a lighter yet still significant note, according to Dominos, Paris Hilton is also the most common fake name used by people calling for pizza deliveries!

Paris is hot property and she makes millions of dollars a year, much of it for personal appearances. 'I went to Austria and got paid $1 million to wave at a crowd and tell them why I loved Austria,' she smiles. Asked why she loved Austria, she said, 'Because they pay me $1 million to wave at crowds!' You can see her logic. The minimum wage debate is never one that's going to interest Paris to a huge extent: she can get paid up to £150,000 for a 20-minute appearance at parties. 'If it's in Japan, I get more,' she grins. People love Paris; she has become such an obsession for her fans, one youngster has described herself as a 'recovering Paris Hilton addict'. She said, 'I love everything from her outfits to her attitude.'

Yes, Paris makes staggering amounts of money for her work but there must be so many heirs and heiresses across the globe that are simply sitting on their backsides, waiting to inherit a fortune. Not Paris. 'I'm trying to build an empire. I don't want to be known as this Hilton girl my whole life. I want to make my own name. I work very hard. I think I'm one of the most hard-working people in the business. I get up every morning at 6 o'clock. I'm on the phone, I'm on the set, doing a photo shoot... I haven't had free time in, like, two years. It's hard, it's a lot of work, but I love it. But people think I don't do anything.' Indeed, never let Paris hear you even describe her as an heiress. 'I think it's retarded,' she says of the description. 'They call me Paris the Heiress. I was going to go to school to study hotel management, but I don't want to be behind a hotel desk. My sister, she's really into all that. I'm more of an artsy person. I'm getting ready to record my album, I have my modelling and acting.'

A role model for women across the world, she has transcended her privileged existence to have the common touch with those who look up to her. Never one to sneer at those who adore her, Paris instead encourages every single one of them to feel good about themselves and to feel that she and they have plenty in common. 'No matter what a woman looks like, if she's confident, she's sexy,' she smiles. 'Doesn't matter what colour hair you got, or your eyes. If you have confidence, you're a nice person, you're sweet and you're funny, I think that's sexy.' In fact, despite her wealthy surroundings, Paris has often displayed the fun-loving, positive, hedonistic outlook on life that is normally associated more with working-class people. Anyone who has seen the time she has for her fans at public events can see there is something democratic about her approach to fame.

Despite rumours of Paris having a boob job in early 2007, she has to the best of our knowledge never turned to the surgeon's knife to try and improve her appearance, unlike so many of her Hollywood contemporaries. 'I like being flat – I think it's hot,' she shrugs. 'I never have to wear a bra. When I was 13, I really wanted a boob job because all my friends started to have boobs and I was the only one who looked like a boy.' Paris keeps it more real than many of the people with whom she shares her social life. Nearly all who come into contact with her attest to her generous and fun spirit. A co-star from one of her films remembers the time they spent together with a warm smile. 'She's very generous and so fun to be with. The best thing about her is that she can totally send herself up. I remember her once joking about how her parents sent her to a holiday camp for rich kids, but she couldn't cope because there weren't enough mirrors.'

Not that Paris really needs a mirror to see her face; all she has to do is open a newspaper or celebrity gossip magazine. These publications are voracious in their appetite for the latest story about her and never have they been greedier for her than when that infamous video of Paris in bed with Rick Salomon was leaked in 2003. Millions around the world switched on their computers to see the footage as it pinged around cyberspace; journalists sharpened their pens to write about the latest development and her critics stood rubbing their hands in glee. Finally, they believed, Paris's time was up.

Having accepted that Paris would fulfil Andy Warhol's prediction that in the future, everyone would be famous for 15 minutes, Paris's envious detractors are confused and not a little upset as she keeps stretching her time in the spotlight further and further beyond the quarter of an hour that the pop-art guru prescribed. Therefore, what happened after the sex video leaked must have been both a shock and a bitter disappointment to each and every one of them. Rather than holding her manicured hands up and saying, 'OK, I look really silly so I'm leaving public life to go and hang out in Daddy's swimming pool for the rest of my life,' she instead turned the scandal to her advantage and bounced back stronger than ever. In truth, the affair cemented her public profile, if anything. Her detractors were so disappointed by this that they claimed she set the whole thing up as a publicity stunt. They just don't give up, but then in a far more admirable way neither does Paris.

Not only is she a born survivor, as her friends have attested Paris also has an exceptional ability to make fun of herself. Much of her performance in *The Simple Life* was her hamming it up for the camera, playing up to the 'dumb It-girl' image she knows many have of her. '*Simple Life* is a reality show and people might assume it's real. But it's fake. All reality shows are fake basically. When you have a camera on you, you are not going to act yourself,' she explains. 'So before I started the show I thought I'd make a character like the movies *Legally Blonde* and *Clueless* mixed together, with a rich girl all-in-one. Even my voice is different, and the way I dress is different from me in real life. It's a character I like to play. I think it's carefree and happy. The public think they know me but they really don't.'

The same high-esteem and sense of fun was behind her hilarious, self-deprecating appearance on *Saturday Night Live* in the wake of the sex-tape scandal. She has also suggested to a New York storage firm that they advertise with the slogan, 'Your closet's so shallow it makes Paris look deep'. The co-author of her official autobiography admits she was blown away by how Paris could poke fun at herself. One wonders whether any of Paris's critics would ever have even a hope of becoming as aware of themselves to the same extent Paris has, let alone the ability to make so much fun of themselves in front of the world.

We all love to chat about Paris and her life. For their March 2007 edition, gay magazine *Attitude* interviewed celebrity couple Richard Madeley and Judy Finnigan. During the interview, they were asked what they thought of Paris, whose look-a-like Chantelle had won the previous year's *Celebrity Big Brother* on Channel 4. The following exchange took place:

R: 'She looks like Chantelle.'

J: 'Yes, that's because Chantelle made her living as a Paris look-a-like.'

R: 'You don't see pictures of Chantelle now.'

J: 'There was one at the weekend.'

R: 'That was Paris Hilton.'

J: 'It was Chantelle! I don't understand what it is with Paris Hilton. I mean, why?'

R: 'Because she does it.'

J: 'Does what?'

R: 'Has sex. And flashes her pubes, whatever it takes… she's a Yes girl.'

J: 'She's very rich, she doesn't need to.'

R: 'But she does; she's an addict to publicity usually with a sexual connotation.'

J: 'You're very odd, Richard, I don't know where you get these ideas from.'

R: 'Probably the gossip columns like you do. I'm right, aren't I?'

J: 'You don't know what you're talking about. I never knew you were a Paris Hilton expert.'

Whether Richard is a Paris Hilton expert or not, this was an entertaining exchange similar to those that must take place at water-coolers and in bars, hairdressing salons and homes all over the world most days of the week. The one thing that unites Paris's fans and critics is that we are all utterly fascinated by her. Madeley is correct in that a lot of the publicity that surrounds Paris has a 'sexual connotation' but that is not something she engineers. Many of the men she has been linked to have been nothing more than good friends. The truth is that Paris enjoys the company of men as friends and she has given up caring that everybody assumes that any man she speaks to, she is also sleeping with.

That said, those men who do get involved romantically with Paris need to accept from the start that she is not going to play the doting, dependent wife role. 'I'm a woman who makes her own money and doesn't depend on a man. I can marry a plumber and it wouldn't matter.' Money cannot buy you love but it sure can buy you independence and Paris stands proudly on her own two feet. Not that she is in any sense immune to the charms of the male of the species and they are pretty fond of her, too. 'When guys get to know me, they realise I'm very different to how they thought I would be,' she says. 'They like that I'm really sweet. I want a guy that I can hang out with and have fun. I like men who have a lot of character and also men with a great sense of humour. I love to laugh and have a good time with a guy. I love walks on the beach. A quiet dinner at a small cosy restaurant. Having serious conversations and not just talking crap. I also want a man I can trust.' The domestically minded Paris also enjoys cooking. 'I can cook feasts, everything. I can make the biggest breakfasts.'

The sheer level of the media's obsession with Paris Hilton can be seen not only in the huge stories they run about her but rather in the smaller stories. Like when a simple visit to a fast food joint by her became a story in a leading newspaper. The quotes from an eyewitness to this apparently earth-shattering event were unintentionally amusing and revealing. 'Paris was shoving fries into her mouth at the counter while she waited for her food. It was unbelievable.' (Eating fries at a fast food counter – unbelievable!) 'She must have been hungry.' (You'll find that visitors to fast food restaurants often are.) 'She was juggling eating, talking on her mobile and fiddling with her shoes – all at the same time.' (Hold the front page!)

Likewise, when she visited Sydney in December 2006, her trip generated more news items than any other event apart from Saddam Hussein's execution. In total, the Australian media devoted more than 3,000 stories to the fact Paris was in town for a few weeks. Can there be a human being on the planet who has not heard of her? (Incidentally, Paris was once asked how she would describe herself to such a person. She replied, 'I'm blonde and tanned and normal-sized! I'm sweet, shy, funny, have a big heart and I'm nice – and I like to eat.')

If some of the coverage of Paris seems out of this world, then one newspaper story about her was literally so. 'PARIS A REAL SPACE CADET' screamed the *Sunday Mirror*, 'EXCLUSIVE – SHE'LL GO INTO ORBIT ON BRANSON ROCKET.' The story went on to reveal that she has signed up with Sir Richard Branson's Virgin Enterprise rocket, which will from 2009 offer regular commercial space flights from their US base in the Mojave desert. 'You'll literally be out of this world,' said a Virgin spokesperson. People close to Paris say she is a huge fan of the *Star Wars* film series and is thrilled by the idea of going into space. Given the lofty level of Paris's ambition, a trip into outer space seems entirely fitting for her.

However, that ambition is definitely matched with intelligence and a sharp mind. Many people will always assume that a beautiful blonde girl is stupid. If she comes from a wealthy background, the temptation to paint her as an 'airhead' or even an 'heirhead' becomes almost irresistible to some sour onlookers. However, Paris has made such a success of so many business ventures that it is very clear that she's far from stupid. Wise beyond her years, she once told an interviewer that she feels like she is much older than she is. How old, she was asked? 'Like, 40,' she answered.

Her repeated driving offences in 2006 and 2007 were

not, however, her wisest moments and she will have to draw on her wisdom and strength to bounce back from the controversy and resultant jail sentence. Only a fool would bet against her managing just that, though. Paris was once asked if it makes her laugh when people assume she is stupid. 'Yeah, I'm laughing all the way to the bank,' she replied. Typical Paris: defiant, successful and always enjoying the last laugh. This woman will not be beaten and it is fair to say that whatever fate throws at her, we'll always have Paris.

1

A STAR IS BORN

On 17 February 1981, in a New York hospital, a star was born. You've come to know her as Paris Hilton but in the early years of her life, the girl who went on to achieve global fame was nicknamed Star by her mother and father. Of course, many parents give an affectionate pet name to their offspring during the early years of their lives but few can have come up with such a prescient epithet. That she has gone on to live up to it has surprised neither Paris nor her family. 'Ever since I was little, everyone said it would happen, and I always wanted it,' she says. One such person who said it would happen was her maternal grandmother, who told a young Paris, 'You're my Marilyn Monroe. You're my Grace Kelly. You're going to be the most famous woman in the world.'

As we've seen, Paris's every move has been documented by photographers and cameramen.

1

Wherever she goes, the paparazzi follow; a team of them are even parked outside her house all day and night. They have become so much a part of her life that Paris now hears the clicking sound of cameras even when there are none around. 'It's really strange,' she says, 'but I can always hear it. It's scary.' Then of course there was that sex video, more of which later. However, the first camera to be pointed at her was held by her father, Rick, who recorded her birth on to a camcorder. A proud dad, he was prodigious with his family filming; he not only recorded the births of Paris and her three siblings, he also taped those of all of their cousins.

Those interested in astrology will already have noted from her date of birth that Paris is an Aquarian. People born under this sign are expected to be creative, entertaining, stimulating and rebellious. They are also expected to have finely chiselled features and slender figures. One writer said of the Aquarian woman, 'She belongs to everyone and yet to no one'. It all seems entirely appropriate so it's little surprise to learn that Paris believes in astrology. When asked how she keeps up her party-animal lifestyle, she shrugged and said, 'I'm an Aquarius. We Aquarians have a lot of energy.' She has also said, 'Because I'm an Aquarius, I don't care. I'll just dance and have fun.' And why not?

Paris Whitney Hilton was christened at St Patrick's Cathedral on Manhattan's Fifth Avenue. The largest Catholic cathedral in the United States, this Gothic Revival building is an Upper Midtown institution and a mere saunter away from the cathedrals to capitalism like Trump Tower, the Waldorf-Astoria and other places that would later play significant parts in her life. Indeed, the sheer scale of architecture in Manhattan makes it a most Paris Hilton city – tall, proud and slim, the skyscrapers are as ambitious and breathtaking as Paris herself. The cathedral had a family heritage: her great-grandfather Conrad – who died two years before Paris was born – had knelt at the same church after celebrating the Waldorf-Astoria Hotel's 25th anniversary in 1918. Back then he was giving thanks for 'the all-American right to dream with the actual possibility of seeing that dream come true'.

Conrad Hilton had good reason to be thankful. The founder of the Hilton hotel company, his story of ambition, determination, adventure and success is the very stuff that the American dream is based on. As *Fortune* magazine put it: 'He created the hotel industry as we know it today.' While he was enlisted in the army during World War One, Conrad planned to join his father, August Halvorsen Hilton, who was born in Norway and emigrated to the USA when he was 10 – in his grocery business. But when his father was killed in a car accident, Conrad was forced to reconsider his plans. Once the war ended, he decided to try and enter the banking industry. In 1919, while looking for a bank in Texas, he attempted to check into the Mobley Hotel in the town of Cisco. He had to wait in a long queue for a room and when he realised how in-demand the two-storey red-brick hotel was, he asked the owner if he was willing to sell the business. The good news was that it was for sale; the bad news was that he had just seven days to raise the $50,000 asking price.

Rushing round to family, friends and — quite possibly — fools, he managed to raise the funds required. Or so he thought: the day before the deal was due to go through, one of his friend's cheques bounced and the deal seemed doomed. Refusing to give up, he convinced a bank to loan his friend enough funds to cover the bounced cheque and the deal went through. Conrad once said, 'Success seems to be connected to action. Successful people keep moving. They make mistakes, but they don't quit.' As we'll see, these are not the only sentiments he uttered that Paris seems to have — consciously or not — adopted in her own life. As for Conrad, he was good as his word and kept moving: this was the first deal in what became the iconic, billion-dollar Hilton Hotel empire.

Conrad quickly cleaned up the building and instilled in his employees a renewed sense of pride and motivation. With such demand for rooms at the hotel, he closed the dining room and divided it into a series of bedrooms. Profits rocketed. He followed the same principles at the hotel he bought four months later, The Melba in Fort Worth, and all the other subsequent hotels he bought. Within four years of buying The Mobley, this incredible man owned 520 hotels.

The Mobley Hotel deal had been secured in dramatic last-minute fashion and when he bought his most prestigious business to date, Conrad again only made the deal by the skin of his teeth. He believed he had enough funds to buy the Waldorf-Astoria Hotel and was an hour away from sealing the deal. However, with less than 10 minutes left before the deadline, one of his partners withdrew their funds. Suddenly, Conrad was $500,000 short and his dream of buying his most glamorous hotel to date seemed in tatters. However, in the closing minutes of the deal he miraculously managed to find all the funds required and the hotel was his.

In 1957, Conrad published a book called *Be My Guest*. In the book, he identifies and lists the '10 ingredients which must be blended in each and every one of us if we are to live successfully.' This lifestyle list was echoed several decades later when Paris published her own book *Confessions Of An Heiress – A Tongue-In-Chic Peek Behind The Pose*. In her book, she lists 23 instructions on 'How To Be An Heiress' and also '12 Things An Heiress Would Never Do', and even 'Three Things Most People Think An Heiress Shouldn't Do But I Think They Should'.

However, Conrad's 10 ingredients for success could just as easily apply to Paris's life. The first is 'Find your own particular talent'. He writes, 'Don't worry about what you haven't got in the way of talent. Find out what you have!' Paris has followed this doctrine herself. Never has she attempted or claimed to be a deep-thinker or philosophical heavyweight; instead she has concentrated on what she has got and has been rewarded for that.

Next up in Conrad's list is 'Be Big: Think Big. Act Big.

Dream Big.' Has Paris ever done anything by half? No, she has always thought big and dreamed big. Whether it is her glorious birthday parties or opulent entries to social events, she is always thinking big. Then, writes Conrad, 'Be honest'. Paris is as honest as they come: whatever her critics say, she's always been true to herself and others. The next Conrad tip is as Parisesque as they come: 'Live with enthusiasm'. Whether it's her tireless partying or tireless work, Paris is as enthusiastic as they come. 'If you have enthusiasm for life you cannot ever know an inactive time of life.' Paris has proved that sentence true time and time again.

Following this on Conrad's list is 'Don't let your possessions possess you.' Of course whether it is expensive jewellery or top-class outfits, Paris has always been a major consumer type. 'Don't worry about your problems,' is the next one. For all the media attention that has been focused on her for many years, Paris has never been one to follow the trend of self-pitying interviews that are so popular among modern celebrities like Robbie Williams. Even when life has dealt her a harsh hand, she has remained as positive as she can. She would never insult her adoring fans by complaining about how life is for someone as wealthy and fortunate as her.

Number seven on Conrad's list is 'Don't cling to the past. Not through regret. Not through longing.' Again, this is very Paris. 'It is wisdom to profit by yesterday's mistakes. It is fatal to hang onto yesterday's victories.' This could almost be Paris speaking. Profiting from mistakes?

When footage of her having sex with Rick Salomon was leaked via the Internet, Paris turned what could have been a career-ending tragedy into a springboard for further success. Not hanging on to victories? Paris is never satisfied with her lot and is always pushing forward.

'Look up to people when you can – Down to no one,' continues Conrad's ten commandments. Despite her enormous wealth, fame and success, Paris has never looked down on people – aside from the odd joke about soup kitchens on *The Simple Life*! 'Assume your full share of responsibility for the world in which you live,' he writes, adding: 'The whole purpose of democracy is for the participation of the individual.' In November 2004, Paris lived up to this principle when she participated in Sean 'P. Diddy' Combs' Vote Or Die campaign, to encourage youths to vote in the Presidential election. The final tip in Conrad's list is 'Pray consistently and confidently.' Although she has never been one to wear her religion on her sleeve, Paris has often thanked God for good things that have happened to her.

Conrad's personal life was just as eventful as Paris's. He married three times – first in 1925 to Mary Barron who he first spotted at Mass one Sunday morning. They had three children – including Paris's grandfather William Barron – before divorcing in 1934. Eight years later, Conrad married again, this time to Zsa Zsa Gabor, the actress and socialite. Gabor said that her new husband was 'a wonderful lover, virile, well-endowed and masterful'. She was 17 at the time and Conrad was 61. The marriage lasted just four years but this was a lifetime when compared to some of Gabor's other marriages, one of which lasted just a day.

Colourful stuff and the same description can be applied to the life of Conrad's youngest son, Conrad 'Nicky' Hilton Junior. Described as 'the marriage and love match of the century' by the press, his marriage to Elizabeth Taylor turned out to be a disappointing experience that lasted just 207 days. Nicky first met Taylor at Mocambo on Sunset Boulevard – the same place that his father had proposed to his stepmother, Zsa Zsa Gabor. Nicky and Taylor soon married, but the shocking secret that he was keeping from his new wife was that he was having an affair – with his stepmother. Closer in age to her stepson than she was her husband, Gabor had embarked on a fling with Nicky and that fling lasted into his marriage to Taylor. That marriage was deeply unhappy.

Racy stuff and also complicated stuff – if you are finding it hard to keep up then you are not alone. However, in her book *Confessions Of An Heiress – A Tongue-In-Chic Peek Behind The Pose*, Paris makes it clear she is proud of her lineage. She also seems approving of Nicky's marriage to Taylor. Pointing out that he was the first of seven husbands she had, she writes 'If you have to be one of a group, it's best to be first.'

Richard 'Rick' Hilton was not the first but the sixth of eight children born to Barron Hilton, Nicky's brother. He grew up in Santa Monica in a grand home overlooking the Pacific. Blond haired, he hung out on the Sorrento Beach and lived the life of riley. When he was 23, and completing his studies at the University of Denver, he met Kathy Richards. Some people work hard and play hard; by all accounts Kathy Richards had been more one to simply play hard in her high school and post-high school years. Her siblings were both in the acting profession. She'd been keen to meet an eligible bachelor for many years – and could there be many bachelors more eligible than Richard? He threw huge, lavish parties at the university and with his gift of the gab, athletic build and family background, he must have represented an incredible catch to young Kathy. Indeed, a biographer of the Hilton family wrote that 'snaring Rick Hilton was like winning the Powerball jackpot'.

All her family were delighted when she announced her engagement to Richard. The pair married on 24 November 1979 in the Church of the Good Shepherd in Beverly Hills. With some very rich parishioners, the Church had become known as 'Our Lady of the Cadillacs'. This was the same church where Nicky Hilton had wed Elizabeth Taylor. That marriage might have ended quickly and ignominiously but Richard and Kathy's was to prove much more successful. 'They have never spent a night apart from each other,' gushes Paris of her loving parents. 'If he goes on a business trip, she goes. They are so in love. My dad is so loyal. My mom is, like, his life and he'll do whatever she wants.' Even a journalist for the notoriously sceptical *Daily Mail* newspaper admitted, having spent time with the couple, that they seemed devoted to each other. 'After 26 years of marriage, I suspect that they wouldn't swap each other for all the hotel chains in the world,' she wrote.

As their first-born child, Paris was a dream come true for Rick and Kathy. Kathy was a young mother; she was only 20 when she had Paris. 'We really grew up together, me and Rick,' remembers Kathy. 'Meeting that young, marrying that young and having the little girls so young.' They lapped up the compliments that other relatives paid to their child. When she was nine months old, Paris was described by one as 'a great big fat pretty baby'. Soon after her second birthday, she was described by another of the Hilton clan as 'gorgeous – her face was incredible, like a porcelain doll'. Paris's aunt, Kyle Richards, said, 'She was the most beautiful baby I had ever seen in my whole, entire life. I was so in love with her. She was such a beautiful baby.' This is more than familial pride: photographs of the baby Paris confirm every word of praise they heaped on her.

Back then Paris's hair was naturally straight. (Thanks to her use of hair-straighteners, it is not widely known that Paris's hair is now naturally very curly). She also had large feet. Her grandfather Conrad also had large feet as a child. He recalled being 'a skinny, shy kid being hauled through town... overwhelmingly aware that his feet, like those of a St Bernard puppy, had reached full growth well ahead of his body, and very often entangled in them'. Paris's feet are now a size 11 and many designers have to make shoes especially for her. When asked how she feels about her big feet she was less loquacious than her great-grandfather: 'It sucks'.

At the age of two, Paris first met the girl who was to play an important part in her life. The pair would become globally famous, star together on a reality television show, and their rollercoaster relationship would become the source of fascination for journalists everywhere. 'We've been best friends since we were two years old. I've don't have any other friend I've had as long as her. She's my sister,' says Paris. That girl is, of course, Nicole Richie. Born in Berkeley, California on 21 September 1981, Nicole had a turbulent start in life. She says her biological father was Peter Escovedo, a drummer working with legendary music man Lionel Richie, and her mother was one of Lionel's backstage crew. When Nicole turned three, Lionel and his wife Brenda Harvey-Richie informally adopted her. Five years later, the couple legally and formally adopted her.

She admits that she was spoiled by her adoptive parents. 'Their way of making me happy was to say yes to everything I wanted, but I don't think a little girl should have that much freedom.' However, soon after she was formally adopted by them, Lionel and Brenda split up. 'I had the freedom to do it [misbehave] because my parents were going through their divorce,' Nicole now says, seemingly with an air of regret. 'Being a teenager and a girl in Hollywood is tough. You feel like you want to be older. It sounds crazy, but I feel lucky because a lot of my friends were going through drug and drink problems at the same time as me. It was like a bonding process.'

However, before all this there were more innocent times during her childhood friendship with Paris. It was at a nursery at the age of two that Paris first remembers encountering Nicole. They were taking part in a school dance recital and the pair were absolutely glamorous and unconventional from the very start. 'We were both dressed up like kitties,' remembers Paris. Nicole too remembers the day well. 'Everyone's doing their tap recital thing and then you see the two of us kicking our feet and doing our own little dance. We do nothing but love each other.' Paris and Nicole went on to the same schools and even shared the same piano teacher.

Paris's earliest memory, however, is of playing with animals at home under the loving and watchful eye of her parents. She was doted upon by both her parents from day one and retains a very close relationship with them. She still speaks to her mother up to 10 times every day and also insists that to this day she remains 'Daddy's little girl'. But when she was three years old, she discovered that she was going to have a rival for their affections. Born on 5 October 1983, Nicholai Olivia Hilton – who quickly became known as Nicky – a nickname that had also been given to her grandfather's brother, Conrad 'Nicky' Hilton. There was absolutely no sibling rivalry towards her younger sister from Daddy's little girl. 'I was never jealous of Nicky after she was born,' remembers Paris. 'I was happy to have someone close. So many of my friends were 'only children', and many of them had divorced parents – so I definitely knew how lucky I was to have a sister and both parents around at the same time.'

The sisters were the real golden girls. When Aunt Kyle walked along with the two young sisters, strangers would stop her 'every five seconds' and dote over how beautiful they were. Not that they had identical personalities. Paris's lifelong friend, Kimberly Stewart, recalls a difference between the Hilton girls. 'Nicky was always very quiet and shy. Whereas me and Paris were loud and obnoxious.' Their mother prefers to see them differently. 'You know what Paris is really like?' she once asked. 'She is like Bambi. She is like a little deer. Nicky is an adorable little bunny rabbit.' She repeated the Bambi description when she told a *Daily Mail* interviewer, 'People say to me, Your daughter isn't at all like I thought she was going to be. She's so sensitive. She'll cry at the drop of a hat. She's like a little deer – like Bambi.'

The sisters were very close from the start. They would fight, but not very often. Once, Nicky snitched on Paris when she overheard her swearing. Paris gave her little sister a passionate lecture on loyalty and Nicky never told tales on her again. The pair have a good understanding of each other, even by the standards of siblings. 'The only person who really knows me is Nicky,' says Paris. 'And not many people know this, but my sister is one of the funniest people you'll ever meet.' Living in an exclusive district of Bel-Air in Los Angeles, they had a fun-packed childhood. They would rollerblade around the neighbourhood, jump around on their mum's big bed and even once built a pretend shop in Paris's bedroom. The rollerblading they grew out of, but shopping remains a key passion for both siblings. One of their favourite places to shop is Japan. They turn up to a huge shopping mall, Paris starts at the top, Nicky starts at the bottom, and they meet halfway, having spent thousands of dollars. Paris can also be seen regularly in expensive American clothing stores like Barney's, Tracy Feith, Tracey Ross and Kitson. In England, she loves Harvey Nichols and Harrods and when in Malibu, Paris loves to shop in Planet Blue at the Cross Creek Mall.

As kids they also put on musical shows for their parents. For these shows they would borrow their mum's clothes, make-up and jewellery and mime to songs by Tina Turner, Whitney Houston, Madonna and Prince. Many of the rehearsals for these performances took place at the home of Lionel Richie. Well, it seems a suitable venue. Sometimes, the shows were more sophisticated. At the age of six, Paris would play the violin and piano for her parents. However, the thought of performing for a wider audience terrified her. 'I was the kid in class who couldn't even make a speech because I'd be embarrassed and shy. I couldn't imagine singing in front of a room of people.' Well, she's certainly managed to overcome her shyness as an adult! Her violin practice did not continue for long, though. 'I stopped when I was, like, eight.' However, as a child Paris would fall asleep to the sounds of classical music, which her mum would put on the radio to ease her girl off to sleep. Paris enjoys classical music to this day, particularly when she slips into a luxurious bubble bath.

They would also pretend they were royalty and Paris would naturally be the queen. Similarly, when they played pretend school at home, Paris would always be the teacher. In real life, Paris and Nicky attended the same schools and shared many of the same clothes as children. 'My mom made sure we were always together and we continued to dress alike into our early teens. I think my mom thought it would give us more confidence, and she was right. She always bought two sizes of the same outfit if she liked it, so we wouldn't get jealous of each other's clothes.'

The two sisters complemented each other at school, too. Paris loved art and Nicky enjoyed writing, so the pair would pool their resources when they were doing their homework. They even had different tastes in boys so they never fell out over one. 'My sister rocks and I never have as much fun with anyone as I have with her,' beams Paris. 'The only person who really knows me is Nicky. We'll always be there for each other. She's always proud of me, in the good times and the rough. That's a wonderful thing to know and to have grown up with.' Paris now admits that if you take pretty much everyone who has ever hurt her in her life, Nicky had warned her about them.

Not that things were always equal, for as a child Paris pulled rank. Every year, Nicky's godfather would give her $100. Paris would dupe Nicky into buying one of her toys from her for $100. Paris would then buy herself a new toy and pocket the difference. She still feels bad about this. They played pranks as a pair, too. They'd made silly phone-calls and leave messages for dogs on other people's answering machines.

Those who think that Paris has never worked in her life will be surprised by how hard she has worked to maintain her businesses and profile. Her knack for business came early on in her life according to her mother. 'Her first job was a summer job, selling cookies. We would make the cookies and she would go outside and sell them! She would be so embarrassed to be reminded. Juice. Cookies. Gum. Little hair combs.' Although Paris had harboured musical aspirations of some sort since the age of six, it was working with animals that she dreamed of as a child. 'I first wanted to be a veterinarian. Then I realised you had to give them shots to put them to sleep, so I decided I'd just buy a bunch of animals and have them in my house instead,' she says. 'When I was a child, I wanted to visit every dog pound and adopt every dog that was going to be killed.'

'Paris had every animal you could think of as a child,' a relative recalled. She had so many ferrets, dogs, cats, it would be nothing for her to stick a mouse in your purse and wait for a reaction when you opened the purse and there was a big rat in there with a huge tail hanging out.' She called one of these ferrets Farrah the Ferret, after her cousin Farrah Richards. Paris also collected frogs and snakes and boasts, 'I was a tomboy. I loved digging tunnels in the backyard.'

When she was 10 years old, Paris had her first moment

of fame when she appeared in the low-budget independent film *Wishman*. Directed by Mike Marvin, its lead character is Basie – a man who collects junk. He is in love with Lily, a woman who is about to get conned out of her money by her greedy lawyer. And then there is the Genie who has lost his bottle and seeks Basie's help. Paris appeared only in passing, her character is listed as 'a girl on the beach'. She appeared alongside younger sister Nicky, who had the same part. This was not the most prestigious of cinematic moments but it was a first step for Paris, into a world she would be spending a lot of time in the future as her billing went up and up the ladder until she could touch the 50-foot white letters of the Hollywood sign.

Paris also has two younger brothers called Barron and Conrad IV, and both of Paris's parents had many siblings, so she is not short of cousins. Her father has five brothers and two sisters and on her mother's side alone, she has 10 cousins, all of whom grew up in Los Angeles. Far from suggesting that she was an isolated, spoiled youngster, childhood photographs of Paris show her happily surrounded by other young members of the clan. At Easter time, Paris's parents would put on quite a show for their children. Their enormous garden would become the scene of an extra special Easter-egg hunt. There would be chocolate eggs, plastic eggs and even some hard-boiled eggs. Some of the plastic ones would contain money and Paris would gravitate towards these. The parents would also buy live yellow chicks, ducklings and bunnies.

Christmas, too, was a very big deal for the Hiltons. Paris remembers that her mother began to decorate for Christmas straight after Hallowe'en. 'She thought she was Mrs Claus,' quips Paris. 'It was my favourite time during childhood and it still is now. I love Christmas and my decorations stay up from the end of November until Valentine's Day practically!' she recalls. Each room in the mansion had its own Christmas tree and the whole experience was 'wild'. She jokes: 'When Santa came to our house, he was a Beverly Hills Santa, in a red Mercedes!'

In later years, Kathy hired Dr Christmas to help ensure the festive season really went ahead with a bang. Dr Christmas's real name is Bob Pranga; he has dressed the homes of Nancy Reagan, Carrie Fisher and Kate Hudson among others, and has a reputation for intense attention to detail. However, it was Kathy who noticed one detail that was out of place. 'Paris's stocking is too far away from the others,' she complained to Pranga. 'It looks like she's set apart from the other children.' Heaven forbid!

One of Paris's passions in life is changing her hairstyle as regularly as possible. She has gone from choppy bobs to long hair and even once had a Gwen Stefani-style Mohican. She loves the relaxing atmosphere of hair salons and enjoys the attention that her hairdresser gives her. Las Vegas salon operator Michael was Paris's first colourist at Jose Eber's salon in the Two Rodeo centre in Beverly Hills, when she was 13. 'Her mom said, "Keep it natural",' he recalls, 'but two months later we were bleaching it out because Paris kept wanting it blonder and blonder, until she was platinum. Even at that age, she knew what she wanted. I told her mom, "You've got to get her into modelling," and she said, "Michael, she's going to grow up fast enough".'

But just how fast? It has been rumoured that Paris got her first credit card at the age of nine. She disputes this and insists in her book that she was 'more like 19' when she got her first 'flexible friend'. Elsewhere, she has put the figure at 17, and she has also disputed reports that she received $100 a week in allowance at the age of 13.

She insists that her parents were extremely strict. 'We had to check in with them like 10 times a day. I had a curfew of midnight until I was 17. People think my parents let us do whatever we wanted, but that wasn't true at all, trust me. I got punished as much as anyone.' She later added, 'My parents always taught us to be humble. We're not spoiled.' Her mother concurs with Paris's account. 'She says I drove her crazy with rules. She says she became rebellious because I was so controlling. She warned me, "Don't be like that with Nicky". She may have had a very good point there. You can't box someone in like that.' Rick's belief was that all family members must 'row their own boat' and not just depend on the family fortune. Paris certainly lived up to his expectations as she grew up.

A major part of her growing-up process happened when Paris was 15, when she is believed to have lost her virginity to Randall Gene 'Randy' Spelling. The son of a legendary television producer, Spelling was born in Los

Angeles, California on 9 October 1978. He has starred in a number of shows and films including *Beverly Hills, 90210* and the reality show *Sons Of Hollywood*. According to Spelling, he and Paris made love for the first time around the same time that the Hiltons first moved to New York. 'We were together for like two months,' said Spelling. 'We went to Palm Springs once for the weekend, and we couldn't check into the hotel under her name because her grandma was looking for her. She was like 15. I was 17. And what do you know, I hear this knock-knock on the door, and I look out and her grandma's there. And then I look out the window and I see Paris in a full-on dress with a suitcase running down the golf course. We broke up like a week later.'

In 2007, Spelling's agent added weight to the story. 'Randy was Paris's number one,' David Weintraub said, 'and her number 50 and number 150.' Paris herself seemed to confirm the story in the same year. While Spelling was hanging around outside a Los Angeles nightclub, Paris approached him. 'She came up to me and she was like, "I want to say hi to Randy",' Spelling said. 'She was like, "Randy took my virginity. I want to say hi"!'

Perhaps as influential an experience in shaping her personality came in less happy circumstances during her teenage years, when Paris spent one year living in Palm Springs with her grandmother who was dying of breast cancer. It was a thoroughly grounding time for Paris, who had not just the illness of her grandmother to try and come to terms with, but the 'simple life' existence of sweating in the kitchen without any maids or help. However, a return to a more glamorous lifestyle was not far away.

In 1996, when Paris was 16, the family moved to New York where Rick opened a branch of his real-estate office. It was a move that young Paris had dreaded. 'I cried,' she recalls. 'I thought I was going to hate it.' In Manhattan, the Hiltons lived in the splendour of the Waldorf-Astoria Hotel. Situated on the exclusive Park Avenue, this 47-storey Art Deco building is widely regarded to be the most glamorous and luxurious hotel in the city. From the moment visitors step into its breathtaking, period lobby with its gorgeous boutiques and beauty parlour, they know they have chosen somewhere very special to stay. Most guests stay there only for a matter of days, a fortnight at the most. Paris and her family can stay there whenever they wish, thanks to her great grandfather Conrad Hilton's skin-of-his-teeth purchase of the hotel. It was here, in the opulence of the Waldorf-Astoria, that Paris developed her taste for a hectic and exciting social life. Living in a grand suite on the 30th floor, Paris and Nicky could order room service at the click of a finger. The gourmet food would arrive quickly on an elegantly decorated tray.

Not that this was the only attention she attracted. 'In Los Angeles there wasn't any attention when I was at high school. But I moved to New York when I was 15 and that's when it all started. I loved Marilyn Monroe and Madonna.

They were strong influences on me. They knew how to become icons. I realised that's what I wanted to be.' She's always been a fan of New York — even using the city's subway system. She adores the confused expressions on the faces of fellow passengers when they see the beautiful heiress slumming it on the subway. However, she does complain that the subway smells of pee so it would be incorrect to describe her as a regular user.

The cheeky sisters would sometimes put pillows in their beds so it looked like they were asleep and sneak out. Not that all their socialising was done in secret. The pair would also attend exclusive parties at the hotel with their parents, and they would also pop up at other functions around Manhattan. Paris loved eating at the Mr Chow and Le Cirque restaurants, which she first went to as a baby. She has since returned to both places to celebrate subsequent birthdays. Those days have become something of a legend but Paris is keen to play them down to an extent. 'It wasn't that crazy,' she insists. 'Any kid who was, like, 16 and allowed into clubs and was invited would go. But we'd go and the media would tell the story 10 times worse. All I was doing was dancing in a club! Who cares?'

However, time offers perspective and Paris does have an understanding of where the fascination came from. 'I moved to New York when I was 16, and all of a sudden everyone started paying attention and talking. I didn't do anything, I was just going out. I think, maybe, there were two sisters and no one had ever seen anything like that in that social scene. I think it's like a dream fantasy people have of heiress sisters. And it is!'

Yet in later years Paris was less enthusiastic about her early social life and there is a hint in her words that even back then she was feeling a little jaded by many of her contemporaries. 'I've been going out since I was 16 and it gets old,' she sighs. 'The same people – lame. It's not cool, these people who have no jobs, who are all losers, basically. Except for my friends.'

The first school she attended in Manhattan was the Professional Children's School. A liberal institution, it was founded in 1914 to encourage children to pursue careers in the arts, entertainment and sporting fields. Under the motto 'Supporting The Arts, Celebrating The Mind'. The likes of *Star Wars* actress Carrie Fisher, *Home Alone* kid Macaulay Culkin, actresses Christina Ricci and Scarlett Johansson and pop singer Anastacia have been through its exclusive doors.

But the main school Paris attended in Manhattan was The Dwight School. 'Use your spark of genius to build a better world.' It's an extravagant motto for an extravagant institution. Founded in 1880 by Julius Sachs of the Goldman Sachs banking family, The Dwight School has long enjoyed an international reputation as a prestigious establishment. Once the school of choice for the German Jewish aristocracy of Manhattan's Upper East Side, it has in recent times included a mix of students from over 30 different countries. Down the years, its alumni has been joined by Fiorello LaGuardia who went on to become

Mayor of New York City, Herbert Lehman, later Governor of New York, the reputable author Truman Capote, and Julian Casablancas, Nick Valensi and Fabrizio Moretti who went on to become three-quarters of rock band The Strokes.

Nevertheless, for all its global and celebrity prestige Dwight is not without its local critics. During the period when Paris attended, the school was known in Manhattan circles as the dumping ground for troublesome spoiled kids. A clever acronym was coined at this time, too: Dumb White Idiots Getting High Together. Horrified by the growing number of jokes, the school jumped into action to restore its battered reputation. It expelled the most obvious offenders and opened a drug-abuse prevention programme. Slowly it restored itself to somewhere near its former glory in the eyes of the world.

It was within the walls of this institution that Paris spent the sophomore and junior years of her high school education. She left at the age of 17 and was sent by her mother to London, where she was taught by a private tutor. While in the English capital, she resided at the Hilton hotel on Park Lane. She never attended university but did spend a while studying fashion in Los Angeles. 'I started working straight from school,' she told an interviewer. 'So I didn't go to college… I don't need to.' Her mother Kathy was disappointed about this. Meanwhile, Nicky attended the Convent of the Sacred Heart in Manhattan's Upper East Side and went on to the Fashion Institute of Technology and Parsons School of Design in New York.

Around this time, Paris also got interested in sport. 'I love ice skating,' she once told a somewhat surprised journalist. 'I play ice hockey too. I've been playing since 10th grade. Hockey is not so rough if you play it with girls. You're not supposed to check people. I don't know what the position I play is called; we always change positions. Not goalie, definitely not goalie. Usually I do score a lot of goals though. I really do love ice skating, have always just loved to skate.'

Other schools attended by Paris included The Marywood-Palm Valley School in California, the Canterbury School in Connecticut and Buckley School in Utah. Kimberley Stewart, friend of Paris and daughter of Rod Stewart, remembers, 'At Buckley, all the guys loved Paris.' She and Paris would hitch their skirts up so they sat a little bit higher than other pupils. They say schooldays are the best days of your life but it is fair to say that this is not a sentiment Paris shares. Her aunt, Kyle Richards, reveals that the girl who sang about jealousy on her first album suffered bullying alongside her sister from envious classmates.

'They're beautiful, they're rich, they have the last name Hilton. They're tall, they're skinny, they're going to get picked on. There was jealousy. I had to... straighten some people out because she was definitely picked on,' she said. 'People would hear the last name and she was always a beautiful girl and that doesn't make for making a lot of friends with girls. She always had this attitude that she didn't care what people thought but she definitely did.'

However, like many of those who are bored at school, Paris was ready to move onwards and upwards – and then some. What would be the next step in the amazing life of Paris Hilton? 'Ever since I was three I've been going to fashion shows,' she once told an interviewer. She'd be quickly going to and starring in many, many more.

2

'THAT'S HOT!

I t's true that Paris was lucky to be born into such a successful and rich family. Her number one tip on how to be an heiress is: 'Be born into the right family.' However, she was just as fortunate in her timing. At the turn of the century, as Paris was reaching her late-teens, the cultural climate shifted considerably in favour of the celebrity. In the 20th century, newspapers had begun to run more and more gossip columns and satellite television had ensured that more broadcast time was concerned with what the stars were up to. Even so, these were just the forerunners for the absolute fame frenzy that would explode in the 21st century. Perhaps this timing was written in the stars for the girl they call Star: the dawning of the age of Aquarius was, after all, meant to happen at the end of the 20th century.

Although launched in 1999, *Heat* magazine – which

had a quiet first year with disappointing sales — personifies the 21st century celebrity culture perfectly. Over 500,000 people read the British magazine's irresistible blend of celebrity news, gossip, fashion, arts reviews and television listings every week. For all those who worship at the altar of celebrity, *Heat* is their sacred text. Celebrity news shows such as the BBC's *Liquid News* only fanned the flames.

The magazine's rise coincided with the dawn of reality television. In 1999, ITV show *Popstars* put together Hear'Say, the first reality television band, and this show was quickly followed by first *Pop Idol* and then *The X Factor*. Throw *Big Brother* into the mix and suddenly the media was awash with people who were, it was said by some, to be 'famous for being famous'. Such celebrities were not entirely unheard of before; It-girl Tara Palmer-Tomkinson had been discussed in similar terms throughout the 1990s. But now there seemed to be hordes of them. And hordes from every social background — for every posh Tara Palmer-Tomkinson there was a working-class Jade Goody. Some sneered at this development; others welcomed it as a democratisation of fame, a partial and belated vindication of Andy Warhol's prediction that in the future 'everyone will be famous for 15 minutes'.

Across the pond in America, exactly the same developments were taking place. *US Weekly* magazine was relaunched in the early 21st century, and every Friday it hits the newsstands with the same sort of content that

Heat gives British readers. Around the same time, the launch of the E! Entertainment Television network replicated a similar approach on the small screen. More and more pages and more and more airtime was simply gagging to be filled. Then there was the worldwide Web, with celebrity sites like PopBitch and TMZ starving for celebrity gossip. Into this vacuum sauntered Paris Hilton, reaching the end of her teenage years and keen to live the dream of so many girls her age and become a star. However, she had no intention of retiring shyly once her 15 minutes were up.

Paris's desire for fame and the media's need for more and more celebrities was a match made in heaven, and Paris has been a mainstay in the media across the world for many years. One of her most iconic and most talked-about media moments came early on in her career and with a more long-running outlet than those already mentioned. *Vanity Fair* magazine has always had a knack for a controversial photo-shoot. In August 1991, the glossy monthly featured a naked, pregnant Demi Moore on its cover. Images of actor Mike Myers dressed as a Hindu deity whipped up such a storm that the magazine was forced to apologise. *Vanity Fair* also once ran a cover featuring Keira Knightley and Scarlett Johansson both naked sitting with a fully clothed Tom Ford. These and other covers have ensured that the magazine has always been much-discussed, with one commentator complaining that they 'felt soiled' when looking at the cover. Paris lists *Vanity Fair* as one of her favourite magazines, alongside *US Weekly*, *In Touch*, *People*, *Vogue*, *Lucky*, *Harper's Bazaar*, *Elle*, *GQ*, *Rolling Stone*, *Entertainment Weekly*, *InStyle*, *Teen People*, *Cosmo*, *Blender*, and *FHM*. She adds that the Abercrombie & Fitch catalogue 'has very cute guys in it'.

In September 2000, Paris, then 19, was joined by 16-year-old Nicky for a raunchy photo-shoot for *Vanity Fair*. It proved a controversial episode even by the standards of the magazine. The provocative images – taken by award-winning photographer David LaChapelle – were eye opening to say the least. In one, Paris is featured wearing a skimpy mesh shirt with nothing underneath. Biting her lip, she flicks her middle finger at the camera. She is also pictured lying on a dirty pavement with her eyes closed and a gentle smile of satisfaction spreading over her face. Her top is pulled down.

The finest shot of all, however – the money shot, one could quite literally say – features Paris standing alongside her sister Nicky. The elder sibling is wearing almost non-existent hot pants and only her blonde hair covers her chest. Her gold necklace says it all: 'Rich'. The controversy that greeted the photo-shoot did not put Paris off working with LaChapelle. 'I love working him,' she purrs in *Confessions Of An Heiress*, 'He's a genius!' His work has certainly divided opinion. 'David LaChapelle is as creatively fertile as 1930s' rule-breaker Salvador Dali... He delights in taking sex and voyeurism and giving them an outrageous, unmistakably contemporary twist,' said *Interview* magazine. However, *New York Magazine* was not so enamoured. 'David LaChapelle should have his artistic licence suspended,' it snapped.

Love him or hate him, his pictures of Paris were worth a thousand words, but more words than that were including in the accompanying article. Written by Nancy Jo Sales, it painted a picture of a pair of the pair as pampered, wild rich kids. 'Of all the girls in gossip land, people gossip the most about the Hilton sisters,' she wrote. Friends of the sisters were quoted claiming that the girls were childish, spoiled and very snobbish. In a separate article, one friend said, 'It's like all Paris wants to do is become famous, to wipe out the past, to become somebody else.' When asked what she thought of Nicky, the 'friend' said, 'She's trying to be Paris'. But one friend, Samantha Ronson – later to find fame as a DJ and singer – came out in their defence in the aftermath of the article's publication. 'It's only bitter people who say these things about them,' she insisted.

However, as Paris's It-girl status soared, she became the focal point of the media's most loquacious natterers: by the time she was 19, Paris was already an obsession for the gossip columns of the American press. The *New York Post* was established in 1801, making it one of the United States' oldest newspapers. Based at 1211 Avenue of the Americas in Manhattan, it has an iconic place in the world of tabloid journalism. In 2004, the *Post* received The Hundred Year Association of New York's Gold Medal Award 'in recognition of outstanding contributions to the City of New York.'

Unashamedly populist, one of the paper's most popular features is the Page Six gossip column. The first page that many celebrities turn to in the morning, it is as cutting as it is informed and authoritative. Although in recent years the Page Six column has often appeared on pages 10 and 12 of the newspaper, it has lost none of its scope, bite or brilliance. *New York Post*'s Liz Smith is known as the Grand Dame of Dish and once said of her trade, 'Gossip is just news running ahead of itself in a red satin dress'. She credits – or blames depending on how you look at it – Richard Johnson, the unflappable editor of Page Six, for giving Paris her profile. Smith wrote: 'If you feel like blaming anyone for the rise of Paris Hilton, I've got your man. Rather, *Avenue* magazine for February has him. He is Richard Johnson, the handsomest, best-dressed gossip columnist in history. He's the guy at the helm of Page Six.'

She goes on to say, 'Richard and his beautiful wife, Sessa von Richthofen, are analysed within the pages and Richard talks of how he helped turn Paris into a full-blown phenomenon. Page Six has broken more stories than anyone on this decade's It girl, analysing her both pro and con. At first, it seems, people questioned why Page Six was doing so much in covering (or uncovering) Paris. But now that she's an international celebrity making millions, Mr. Page Six himself says, "I feel our judgment has been vindicated in the court of public opinion."'

Paris wrote in *Confessions*, 'If people read a few tidbits about you in *Vanity Fair* or on Page Six they instantly want to know more. They will want to know everything about you. If there's one thing I've learned, it's this — people need to believe your life is better than theirs.'

It is apt that Paris linked Page Six and *Vanity Fair* because by the time the *Vanity Fair* shoot was published, she was a mainstay of the Page Six column. In her first appearance Paris was described by the Page Six crew as 'our favourite airhead heiress'. It claimed she had a steamy clinch with a grunge singer in the green room of an MTV studio. Just weeks later, they reported that Paris had chased a stretch limo containing some Playboy girls down an LA street. Although it was travelling at least 15 miles an hour, she caught up with it and dived in when a door was opened for her. Soon after this, it reported that she appeared at a karaoke party in skimpy underwear and sang a Madonna song.

Week after week, Paris was on Page Six: bending over in a skimpy red dress and revealing her G-string at Greenwich's Laparue club; being accused of pinching someone's make-up at the Sundance Film Festival; drinking milk through a straw with Brandon Davis, grandson of billionaire Marvin Davis; partying with friends on the Sunset Boulevard; smooching with Jared Leto; writhing round in a string bikini at the Cannes Film Festival; partying hard with Tara Reid four nights in a row in St Tropez.

Paris remembers with joy the first time she saw a photograph of herself in the newspapers. 'I was 16. In the fashion section of the New York Post. Me and my sister. Best dressed.' The press tried to portray both Paris and

Nicky as out of control in these years. Others would see the same behaviour as two young ladies letting their hair down and having a ball — behaviour to be applauded and not derided. At the Sundance Film Festival in Park City, Utah, Nicky allegedly disrupted a live performance from a rock band at an exclusive bash when she refused to withdraw from the stage. Meanwhile, a scantily clad and tipsy Paris was dancing on a table.

Naturally, elder sister Paris was very much the trailblazer of the pair and Nicky the younger sister followed enthusiastically in her wake. Although Nicky was just 16 when reporter Peter Sheridan tracked down the pair in Los Angeles, she was reported to look as old as 25 and to be regularly spotted smoking cigarettes and drinking champagne through a straw. 'Though both Lolitas are under the legal drinking age,' wrote Sheridan, 'the duo launched themselves on America's nightlife with a vengeance… strutting their way past every velvet rope, and into every star-studded VIP room with an open bar.' At a Hugo Boss party, Paris changed her outfit a number of times and then scrambled on top of a coffee table to dance in full view of all present. 'She was kicking over candles and bottles and ashtrays,' said an onlooker. Sounds like a great night.

Meanwhile, documentary producer Peter McAlevey, who was making a film about the Los Angeles club scene, compared Paris to a figure from Swinging Sixties London. 'I've worked with Michael Douglas, Julia Roberts and I've seen people come and go, but Paris has everything,' he enthused. 'She is today's Twiggy'. Not that everyone was so enamoured. One society elder told Sheridan that the pair were 'disgraceful' and added that 'if they had any respect for their families, they would keep their noses clean'. More explicit disappointment in the girls' antics was voiced by Celestine Hines, a fourth-generation Hilton. 'I'm ashamed that Paris and Nicky are related to me,' she said.

Paris had enormous confidence for someone her age, and occasionally that confidence spilled over. At the Las Vegas strip club Crazy Horse, Paris hit the VIP section with a Playboy girl. A male friend of hers was getting plenty of attention from the strippers and Paris is reported to have seen red and hurled abuse at the strippers. Security guards arrived and asked Paris for her ID. 'I don't need ID,' screamed Paris. 'My grandfather built this town! Don't you guys ever read the newspaper? Can you guys even read?'

Paris's exciting It-girl existence was followed every step of the way by the tabloids. Occasionally, exception was taken to the reports. When Page Six gave a colourful description of the outfit worn by Paris at a lingerie party, her mother was quoted as complaining, 'It wasn't a G-string! Paris is the most modest girl!' Given the nature of the *Vanity Fair* photo shoot, modest was not a word that everyone was associating with Paris at this stage. Many people asked how the Hilton parents could have allowed their teenage daughters to take part in such a raunchy photo shoot in a national magazine. As for the magazines, they loved Paris. 'Paris loves the spotlight and the spotlight loves Paris,' said Tina Diname of *Star* magazine. 'When they ask her for a photograph she's like, "Why sure!" She'll stand there for 20 minutes. She's beautiful, she's controversial, she makes good stories and she's rich to boot!'

Looking back over childhood videos of her two girls, Kathy remembered how she would slap make-up on them when they were toddlers. There appears to be an element of regret in her words when she says, 'I was just a kid myself'. She was 21 when Paris was born.

All this fame was bringing Paris plenty of attention, and lots of it came from men. She was about to come to the attention of a very famous and much-desired young man.

3

MODEL BEHAVIOUR

However much of a mainstay Paris became on the *New York Post*'s Page Six, that column cannot claim to have 'launched her' into the world of newspaper gossip. In fact, the first gossipy mention in any newspaper of Paris Hilton came on the pages of the UK's the *Sun* newspaper. On 18 March 2000 the *Sun*'s showbusiness correspondent Victoria Newton published a story about '*Titanic* hunk' Leonardo DiCaprio's nightclub encounter with 'an 18-year-old blonde named Paris Hilton.'

The story reported that 'super-rich Paris, named after the French hotel that is part of the famous Hilton chain founded by her great granddad ... saw Leo in a New York club and danced up to his table. Leo was immediately smitten. Hilton is well-known on the LA club circuit, where she has been spotted partying with stars like actor Christian Slater and Rod Stewart's ex Rachel Hunter.'

This story came out two days before Paris's first appearance in Page Six. Given how many column inches, nay miles, she has commanded ever since, it is a commendable coup that the *Sun* got there first.

Leonardo DiCaprio was hot property. A pin-up for girls across the globe, the Golden Globe winner had shot to superstardom for his roles in films like *Titanic* and *Romeo + Juliet*. When he met Paris, his new film *The Beach* had been out for just a month but it had already taken £25 million at the box-office. The media was awash with talk of 'Leomania'. Like Paris, he is not one of the sort of self-indulgent celebrity to wring his hands and complain about the level of fame he has attained. 'You kidding? I feel very fortunate. A lot of people would love to be in my position. There are so many people out there who are suffering trillions of times more than I could ever suffer, and would love to be me. I am a lucky little bastard.'

A lucky little bastard who was about to get even luckier and hook up with Paris Hilton! 'I like girls who are intelligent, somewhat funny, and pretty with a nice personality,' he says. On the evening in question, one such girl had approached DiCaprio. Paris asked him, 'Do you think I could have a glass of champagne?' It was the start of a beautiful, if short, relationship. The actor visited Paris at the Waldorf Hotel and she made a return visit to him at his Manhattan residence.

Someone close to Paris was quoted as saying, 'Paris is madly in love with him. She has all the money in the world but what she really wants more than anything is to marry Leo. And Leo is very turned on by her.' He was taken by her, too, and reportedly dumped his long-time girlfriend, model Kristen Zang, after meeting Paris. He had been dating Zang – who had also been in relationships with Michael Hutchence and Nicolas Cage – on and off for five years but she was shown the red card after he met Paris (who has denied reports that she also once had a relationship with Cage).

Paris's relationship with Leo lasted just months. However, the pair shared a headline again in June 2005 when DiCaprio was assaulted by a crazed stalker at the home of Paris's ex-boyfriend and video-rat Rick Salomon. Although Paris had no connection with the party, the newspapers noted that both Salomon and DiCaprio had links with her and focused on this fact. It was another sign of how Paris preoccupies the minds of the media and how her every move fascinates them. In 2006, during an interview with *Star* magazine, Paris was asked who her ideal leading man for a film would be. She first dodged the question but did admit that she thought Ben Stiller was really funny and that she also admired Will Ferrell. When asked whether she'd like to star alongside Leonardo DiCaprio, her answer was 'Whatever'.

After the DiCaprio split, Paris was first linked to Edward Furlong. Born in Glendale, California in August 1977, Furlong has starred in a number of films and is best known for his role in *Terminator 2: Judgement Day*. He is also known for a colourful personal life. When he started dating Paris in 2000, he had not long broken up from a five-year relationship with his manager, Jacqueline Domac, which had ended in bitter circumstances. More immediately, he had also just split up with actress Natasha Lyonne, the troubled star of *American Pie*. He had a reputation as something of a party animal and once vomited in front of gossip journalists at a high-profile party.

He was first seen with Paris at the LA club Las Palmas in September 2000. The couple were then spotted on a party, aboard a cruise yacht, which had been thrown by designer Anand Jon. There was an awkward moment when Paris saw Sean 'Puffy' Combs at the party – she had recently slagged him off during a magazine interview. She duly ducked behind Furlong when she spotted Combs and further embarrassment was averted.

However, any awkwardness that night was dwarfed by events at a Playboy party for model Kylie Bax's upcoming pictorial at the Playboy Lounge in Midtown Manhattan. When Natasha Lyonne arrived, she saw red when she spotted Paris, who was now dating her ex-boyfriend. She mooched past Paris and snarled at her, 'You f*cking slut'. Paris approached Lyonne and asked, 'Why are you calling me names when I don't even know you?' Lyonne responded, 'I'm not talking to you.' Then Lyonne turned to her friend and said, 'I'd better get out of her before I do something,' and flounced out of the venue.

Although Paris handled that awkward situation with class and dignity, she was very shaken up by the encounter. 'That was scary,' she told a friend later. 'I felt like she wanted to kill me.' Nevertheless, she kept her cool and stayed at the party where throughout the evening Donald Trump's 22-year-old son Donald Jr was spotted several times admiring her black crop top and hip-hugger trousers. The saucy sod!

Paris and Furlong were then photographed at a *Revolution Magazine*/Diesel party in LA. One publication described Furlong as being 'in an apparent state of free fall' as 'he was dragged like a doll all over the city by Paris'. However, the dragging didn't last for long and by the spring of 2001, the pair had split. Next time Paris saw Furlong, it was at the Whiskey on Sunset Boulevard. He turned up with his new girlfriend and the former couple barely acknowledged each other.

The split had been precipitated the previous autumn when Furlong went into rehab to address his personal problems. While he was there, Paris was said to be dating boxer Oscar De La Hoya, who she had been chatting with on the evening of Natasha Lyonne's hissy fit. Nicknamed the Golden Boy, Mexican-American De La Hoya is considered one of boxing's all-time greats. Following their first meeting, the couple had been spotted together several times, including one occasion when the pair were enjoying a passionate encounter in the back of his limousine. They also took a break together in Las Vegas and dined together at Robert De Niro's Ago restaurant in Hollywood.

She might have been moving in circles dominated by Hollywood royalty in the US, but Paris hung out with some real royalty in Britain in June 2000 when she attended the 18th birthday party of Prince William. 'I've met his father before,' she said before jetting to the UK for the party. 'But I've never met him. He's gotten really cute, though.' The party took place at Windsor Castle in Berkshire, though William – who was studying for his 'A' levels at the time – is understood to have put in only a fleeting appearance. She later purred, "I think Prince William is hot. I've seen him, like, at polo matches.' But asked if she has ever spoken to him, she admitted, 'I'm too shy.'

But if she held a torch for Britain's royal heir, she didn't share the same passions for Britain's then Prime Minister. Asked if she fancied Tony Blair, she answered, 'Who?' After some thought she said, 'Oh yeah... he's like your president?' Then she added, 'I don't know what he looks like.' That said, she has long expressed a preference for British men. 'They're very sweet, there are lots of nice guys out there. They're so polite and I love the accent,' she purrs.

That same year, aged 19, Paris signed with the T Management modelling agency, run by her father's friend the tycoon Donald Trump. 'I wanted to model and Donald was like "I want you at my agency." So now I'm with them and I'm loving it,' she smiled. Naturally, the deal was announced first in the *New York Post*'s Page Six column. 'Paris wants to have a modelling and acting career. I think it is wonderful that she is standing on her own two feet,' T Management president Annie Veltri told the paper.

While with T Management, Paris was coached in how to saunter down the catwalk at fashion shows. So gifted is Paris in the ways of the catwalk that it would be tempting to conclude that seductively sauntering down the catwalk, in that inimitable supermodel manner, comes naturally to her. However, this isn't the case. She was taught how to by Willi Ninja, who also taught a host of models including such luminaries as Grace Jones, Naomi Campbell and Christy Turlington. His work was also the inspiration for the video for Madonna's smash-hit single *Vogue*.

Ninja – whose real name is William Leake – had starred in 1990 documentary about New York's drag balls called, ironically enough, *Paris Is Burning*. Of his work with Paris, he said, 'She's a sweet girl. She's got the power, the money, the beauty, but she really is not as into getting it as she should be. I think her attitude is "I'm Paris Hilton, everyone's paying for my looks and my name, I really don't care." He remembered her turning up at his office wearing expensive casual clothes and carrying a toy dog. He asked her how much the dog cost and she told him it was $4,000. 'How do you get through to somebody that has everything?' he wondered.

Nevertheless, he must have got through to her because soon young Paris was mooching down the catwalks like an established professional. At the February 2001 New York fashion week she appeared at a Catherine

Malandrino show wearing a star-print black-and-white dress. She also glided down the catwalk wearing outfits by Anne Bowen and Lloyd Klein.

She was one of a bevy of new models appearing on the scene at this time, who already had a claim to fame before they hit a single catwalk. Elizabeth Jagger, leggy daughter of Mick Jagger and Jerry Hall, actresses including Michelle Rodriguez and Izabella Miko, singers Mya and Cherokee, Donald Trump's model girlfriend Melania Knauss, and socialites Dayssi Kanavos and Elizabeth Kieselstein-Cord joined Paris at the show. 'Fashion is the new sports arena,' quipped Anand Jon. 'Celebrities add positive friction to the runway.' One reporter wondered whether the next stop for traditional models would be the unemployment office.

One person who didn't put in an appearance was Donald Trump's daughter Ivanka Trump, who was encouraged by her parents to instead spend the time studying and mixing with people closer to her own age. However, there was no stopping Paris who was adjusting to the modelling world like a duck to water and making great waves as she did so. She shared an LA apartment with March 2000 Playmate Nicole Lenz and July 1999 Playmate Jennifer Rovero.

In May 2001, she flew to St Tropez to attend supermodel Naomi Campbell's 31st birthday party. Naturally, this was a star-studded occasion with Donatella Versace, Formula One honcho Bernie Ecclestone, Lady Victoria Hervey and Brazilian football star Ronaldo. Also in attendance that night was a man called Tim Jeffries. Described by one newspaper as 'James Bond meets Kennedy cousin. Mel Gibson meets aftershave model in boxer shorts,' Jeffries had family links to the Green Shield stamps empire and ran a gallery in Mayfair. He had been briefly married to Koo Stark and dated a string of glamorous women including Elizabeth Hurley and Claudia Schiffer. This was getting him quite a reputation: the same article said he was 'fast becoming the playboy of the Western world. Muscled, car-mad and utterly English, he could be the James Bond of the new millennium.'

Paris was wearing sunglasses and dancing on tables at Campbell's birthday bash. However, she still noticed Jeffries and was reported to be keeping a very sharp eye on him throughout the night. The party raged on until dawn, when Paris was seen with her arms around his waist, and with a triumphant look on her face. Whatever happened next didn't lead to anything significant. Just three months later, both Paris and Jeffries attended a fundraising bash at London's Serpentine Gallery. Jeffries – head of the Serpentine Gallery Committee – and Paris were not reported to have paid much attention to each other.

Not that this particular success made her forget where she came from. When Paris turned 21, she celebrated her birthday in the club room above Manhattan's Studio 54. The night was catered for by Le Cirque restaurant. Only family and close friends were invited to the bash where Paris finally drank her first legal glass of champagne, not that she was unfamiliar with bubbly before this.

'I celebrated my own 21st birthday years ago at the original 54,' explained Paris's mother Kathy. Guests included socialites Helen Schifter, Muffie Potter Aston, Dayssi Olarte de Kanavos and Somers White. 'The invitation said funky, but I think that means something entirely different in LA,' said Aston, who, like her friends, was wearing all black. A slide show of photographs of Paris's life was shown. 'Wow. There are a lot of pictures of Paris out there,' said one guest.

There were also a lot of parties out there. The Studio 54 event was the first of five different parties in five different cities thrown by Paris to celebrate her 21st. The other four cities were LA, Tokyo, London and Las Vegas. 'I have friends in each of those places,' wrote Paris in *Confessions*... 'So of course I had to have five different outfits. The travelling didn't bother me; it was worth it to have such a memorable birthday.' The organisation of this party extravaganza was handed to a model agency.

Her penultimate party stop was London, where *In Style* magazine reported: 'She partied at the Stork Rooms with British socialite Lady Victoria Hervey and a gaggle of Euro-catwalkers'. Also in attendance were Alexandra Aitken, daughter of disgraced former Tory minister Jonathan, Tom Parker Bowles, Petrina Khashoggi, producer Nellee Hooper and Enrique Iglesias, Cilla Black and interior designer Nicky Haslam.

Of more note than the guest-list, however, was Paris's unfortunate entrance. Arriving at the club after dinner at Drones, she fell down the stairs in full view of the assembled guests. 'Look – I'm wearing six-inch heels,' she said as she returned to her feet. She has always been able to recover from an embarrassing moment. Once, at a Hollywood party she accidentally stepped into a pond covered by flowers. To make matters worse, she was on the phone at the time.

'I wasn't embarrassed,' she wrote in *Confessions*, 'just a bit scared. I say that when you're in an embarrassing situation, just laugh at yourself. If you get embarrassed, it will only make the situation worse. So I don't get embarrassed. That's for other people. An heiress should never be embarrassed. Anyway, nobody can hate someone who's laughing at herself.' Luckily, the accident didn't result in her flashing too much flesh, for Paris enjoys not wearing too much underwear. 'I find a lot of it shows through your clothes and that looks so tacky. If I do wear any it's a G-string and maybe stockings – they are trashy but in a good way. They look so great you can't help but feel sexy in them.'

Already making great waves in the fashion industry and partying with fashion royalty such as Naomi Campbell, Paris was happy with her progress in this world. However, she was not about to take it too seriously as the next move in her incredible career would attest.

4

GIRL ON FILM

Although Paris was making great waves in the fashion industry, it is a mark of her sense of humour and the fact that she has never taken herself too seriously that her first part in a major Hollywood movie was to be in a film that satirised the world of fashion. *Zoolander* is a silly but funny satire of the fashion world directed by Ben Stiller. For this, his third directorial outing, Stiller hired a host of celebrity cameos for the shooting of the film, which began in September 2000. One of these cameos was Paris.

In *Zoolander*, the world's top made model Derek Zoolander is played by Stiller. An amusingly moronic character, his career is falling apart: a horrendous *Time* magazine profile of him is written by journalist Matilda Jeffries (Christine Taylor), he fails to win his fourth Model of the Year award and then his three roommates are killed in a 'freak gasoline-fight incident'. The final nail in the coffin of his career comes in the shape of a 'walk-off' duel with the hot new model, Hansel (Owen Wilson). Full of despair, Zoolander says, 'I'm pretty sure there's more to life than just being really, really good looking, and I plan on finding out what that is'. To this end he returns to the New Jersey mining town where his father and brothers live. He is rejected by them, too.

Meanwhile, the new Prime Minister of Malaysia is threatening to close down the child labour factories on which the fashion industry is said to rely. Zoolander ends up unwittingly embroiled in a plot to kill the Prime Minister. But he also ends up getting involved in a counterplan to save the Prime Minister, and everyone lives happily ever after. Not least Derek who opens The Derek Zoolander Centre For Kids Who Can't Read Good And Wanna Learn To Do Other Stuff Good Too.

The film suffered at the box office because it came out a fortnight after the September 11 attacks. It was the first comedy to hit the big screen after that tragedy. Indeed, the makers had to digitally remove the Twin Towers of the World Trade Centre from the footage at the last minute. If you look closely during the 2006 film *World Trade Centre*, starring Nicolas Cage, you can see a poster for *Zoolander* in the background of one of the film's early scenes on a Manhattan street. Despite the unfortunate timing of its opening, it quickly picked up as Americans returned to the cinema, wanting to be cheered up. 'New York needs the therapy of laughter,' said Sonia Friedman, a producer of Broadway comedies. 'I have too many people saying this to me for it not to feel true.'

When they did go, audiences enjoyed a film whose cast included a galaxy of stars making cameo appearances as themselves. Donald Trump, Tommy Hilfiger, Lenny Kravitz, David Bowie and Gwen Stefani were among these. As was Paris, whose part was small but whose involvement drew praise from director Stiller. 'She was a great help in figuring out how to do the club scenes,' he smiled. It was in such a scene that Paris appeared in the film. Zoolander arrives at an exclusive party in a club, just as it appears that his career is going to get back on the rails. 'Hey Derek, you rule,' she smiles as he marches triumphantly through the club. 'Thanks, Paris. I appreciate that,' he replies.

Stiller also drew comparisons between the two worlds that Paris was then living in: fashion and Hollywood. 'The fashion industry is no more ridiculous than the movie industry,' he said. 'One of the things they have in common is that people take themselves kind of seriously. We all tend to think the world revolves around us, that we're doing something important. People idolise celebrities. It's just part of our culture.' As for Paris, she was looking up to the celebrity at the centre of the film. 'I'm a big fan of Ben Stiller and I loved the movie *Zoolander*,' gushes Paris. 'I like that really sick, silly humour. And making fun of myself is something I've always been good at. Note to the Farrelly brothers, who are always casting funny, ditzy blondes: I'm available. Call my managers.'

In 2003, Paris appeared in *Wonderland*. Directed by James Cox, *Wonderland* stars Val Kilmer, Kate Bosworth and Lisa Kudrow. It's based on the 'Wonderland murders', the killings of four people in LA in 1981, with a porn star and notorious businessman thrown into the mix. Paris had a 20-second cameo part as a swimsuit-clad party girl on a yacht.

Paris had been working very hard at learning to act. 'I've been doing classes for three-and-a-half years, three times a week using the Sanford Meisner technique,' she revealed. Meisner-trained actors are often very strong on improvisation and spontaneity. Sanford Meisner was an American actor and acting coach who said 'Acting can be fun. Don't let it get around.' His Meisner technique was reportedly studied by a host of stars including James Caan, Robert Duvall, Gregory Peck, Bob Fosse, Jon Voight, Jeff Goldblum, Grace Kelly and Sydney Pollack. Another, very Parisesque, saying by Meisner was, 'You're not going to survive unless after the scene you can go out and get a hamburger and forget about it.'

Much as she enjoyed her cameo roles in *Zoolander* and *Wonderland*, Paris wanted more, more, more. Not just a bigger part, she also wanted to play a character, rather than simply appearing as herself. 'I do not want to be Paris Hilton in every movie. I want to be an actress,' she said. Very soon her dream would come true.

Speaking of dreams, 2001 also saw Paris have one of hers analysed. Lauren Lawrence is a celebrity dreams analyst and former columnist for *George* magazine, the monthly lifestyle title launched by John F. Kennedy Junior in 1995. In 2001 she published a book called *Private Dreams of Public People* that took dreams celebrities revealed having and put them under her expert microscope. Paris had admitted to having a dream where she was driving recklessly in a car, with puppies in the backseat. 'It's like she's being chased in the car, and I look at it as her wanting to be 'chaste',' Lawrence says. 'There is a wish to maintain some kind of morality and ethical standard in her life.'

Whether that was true or not, Paris definitely had a wish to maintain and build on her acting career, following her part in *Zoolander*. 'I've been acting since I was a little girl. Every school play, I was always the lead. When I moved to LA, I knew that's what I wanted to do. I don't care about Oscars and that kind of stuff, and I don't do it for the money. I just do it 'cause I love it and, years from now, I'll have something to show my kids and grandkids.' She found it easy to fit in the acting with her other commitments. 'I love acting a lot, and it's fun to make movies, so I concentrate on that. With my clubs and everything else, all I have to do is talk on the phone and email things. And with my music, I do that at night.'

Appropriately, given that she was blending music and acting, in May 2001, Paris was linked to actor and musician Jared Leto. She was reportedly first spotted smooching with him at Whiskey on LA's Sunset Strip. At this time, he was supposedly in a relationship with actress and former model Cameron Diaz. 'Jared was seen kissing

Paris while Cameron was filming *The Sweetest Thing* in northern California,' said a source. A few weeks later they were spotted in Malibu looking very loved-up. 'I've known Jared for a couple of years,' Paris said at the Paramount Hotel's 10th anniversary party. 'I'm not hooking up with him.' She was, however, linked to him again in 2005 when the *Daily Star* speculated that her happy demeanour at the Usher 'Truth Tour' DVD launch at the Roosevelt Hotel was down to her rumoured hook-up with Leto.

Twice chosen by *People* magazine as one of their 50 Most Beautiful People, Leto was also nominated as one of PETA's (People for the Ethical Treatment of Animals) sexiest vegetarians. He first came to public attention in the television show *My So-Called Life* in which he played Jordan Catalano. He then moved to films, most notably the movie *Requiem For A Dream*. He is also the vocalist in the band 30 Seconds For Mars. Leto has since been linked to sometime friend of Paris, Lindsay Lohan.

As she was determined to do, in 2002, Paris took her acting aspirations one step further when she flew to London to shoot her part in the psychological thriller *Nine Lives*. Filming took place at the Wrotham Park stately home in Barnet and Paris got praise from the crew for her professional approach. Her character Jo is a jet-setting socialite who shops on three different continents in one day. 'She wakes up at dawn, and is in bed by 10 p.m. She gets us food. She's earning her keep,' producer Giles

Hattersley gushed. 'I wanted a bit of the jet-set lifestyle, but she's not delivering,' he then joked.

Director Andrew Green also had praise for her. 'She prepared hard for this. She wanted to impress. She has a screen presence I haven't seen for a long time. Whenever production companies saw what we'd done they said, "Do more Paris, put more of her in".' Paris explained her part. 'My character is supposed to be this socialite – smart and funny, a spoiled jetsetter. That's probably what people would expect. But I'm the complete opposite. They think I'm going to be rude, but I'm just so different.' She told another reporter that during filming she hadn't been out at all. 'I have to get up at six in the morning, but I love London. It's my favourite city in the whole world!'

However, she did manage to bravely step up to the plate and squeeze in a bit of time to party. Her frolics at a party in Marylebone, made quite a splash in the newspapers. 'There were lots of people in the pool and they were all naked. Paris looked the worse for wear, so she might not even remember if she was in the pool or not.' Paris happily confirmed that she was at the bash, saying 'It was a lot of fun.' During the filming she stayed with Giles Hattersley in London. 'For several weeks she filled our spare room with Gina shoes, Juicy tracksuits and a miasma of sickly Guerlain perfume,' he remembers. 'It was like having a Barbie to stay – albeit one with a taste for hard liquor and dubious men. The partying was wild. The hangovers were chronic. Everything was pink.'

Rosie Fellner, who made her name in the classic BBC

comedy sketch show *The Fast Show*, appeared alongside Paris in *Nine Lives*. She remembers wild times with Paris during the film's making. 'The first time we met she had to choose her body double for a shower scene. It was surreal. Girls would come in one by one and we'd say: 'Strip off.' Paris was keeping up a running commentary. "Oh my God, look at that bottom; what horrible boobs." In the end, I convinced her she was better off doing the scene herself, so she could control how much she revealed. With a body double they would try to show as much flesh as possible and everyone would think it was hers.'

Fellner goes on to say that clubs were always calling Paris up, inviting her to things. 'Everything's free. We'd go to places like Chinawhite, full of people like Nicky Haslam and all those It girls, like Lady Victoria Hervey and Laura Parker Bowles. The highlight was being invited to her 21st birthday party at the Stork Rooms in London – Paris was also having parties in Paris, New York, Tokyo and Las Vegas.'

In *Nine Lives*, Tim invites eight of his closest friends to celebrate his 21st birthday with him at his Scottish estate. A snowstorm cuts them off from the outside world but such is the frivolity, nobody minds at first. However, the house has a dark secret locked away in its history. A book tells the story of Murray, an old Scot patriot, who has had his eyes torn out and his house taken away during the English invasion. Murray's spirit is determined to wreak a brutal revenge on the reunited English friends and possesses one of the guests, turning him into a murderer.

This sets up a brutal chain of killings and only one guest survives the ensuing carnage.

An atmospheric film in a beautiful setting, there is much to enjoy for any viewer of *Nine Lives*. But the film was not much of a success. The most positive review of it on the Internet Movie Database (IMDb) says, 'OK – no classic but it isn't THAT bad' which is damning with faint praise, really. Nonetheless, appearing in such a mid-budget film did add a certain trendy edge to Paris's cinematic CV.

And while in England, Paris added another new entry to her CV – under the heading 'Business Interests'. She decided to invest in posh Knightsbridge eaterie The Collection. Going into the deal with Ivanka Trump, she managed to pip actor Hugh Grant to the post. Paris and Trump put £1 million each into the venue – a favourite of celebrity royalty that included Kylie Minogue, Prince and LL Cool J. The *Evening Standard* described the venue thus: 'On the door at The Collection, "face scouts" pride themselves on turning away anyone who doesn't make the grade, while part-time models serve behind the bar and wait at the restaurant. Kylie Minogue entertained guests there after this year's Brit Awards, tiny popstar Prince partied there last month with supermodel Lucy Mans, and Mariah Carey spent Hallowe'en there with guests including Lionel Richie and Missy Elliot.' The paper also predicted a 'battle of the It girls' in the UK once Paris and Trump appeared. It pitted them against Lady Victoria Hervey and Tara Palmer-Tomkinson.

The club's owner, Jay Bolina, said, 'I can't divulge the exact amount in figures but their shares will have a likely value of £1 million at least, for each of them. 'I met Ivanka and Ivana Trump in New York last week to speak about it. Initially we were looking to do it with someone like Tamara Beckwith. But we wanted something a bit more interesting – the Paris and Ivanka connection seemed more fun. I spoke to Hugh Grant about it, but he is keeping to his acting.'

He chose Ivanka and Paris because they are both good-looking, elegant and world-famous. 'They won't be involved on a day-today level but when they are in town they will be able to party in their own place. They're fun, cool and down to earth,' he added. 'Not like these London It girls who are just in it to get photographed. To have someone of substance involved is really nice.'

The next film that Paris appeared in was the short film *QIK2JDG*. Based on Neil Hampton's novel, *Runaway Model*, it features Paris as a strung-out supermodel. After losing her contract with Ford Models, she goes to a club to drown her sorrows but her arch rival comes to pick on her. She starts a fight and ends up with more trouble than she bargained for. The five-minute film, directed by Nick Spano, offered Paris further experience in her acting career.

The same can be said of her part in the movie *Pauly Shore Is Dead*. Pauly Shore is an American actor and comedian. In the film Shore plays himself and fakes his own death in order to revitalize his fading career. It is full of cameos from the likes of Sean Penn, Whoopi Goldberg,

Dr. Dre, Perry Farrell, Fred Durst, Jerry Springer, Montel Williams, Sally Jessy Raphael, Kurt Loder… and Paris. It was only released in Australia but has received some glowing reviews from some quarters.

One of her co-stars remembers that Paris was so in demand at this time that she had to regularly break off to take calls. 'The phone kept going off so filming had to be stopped while Paris chatted to her friends. She hates being disconnected from her social and work scene. It was terribly annoying for the show but in the end they managed to get it in the can.'

With a stake in a posh UK restaurant and further movie roles under her belt, this was an exciting time for Paris. Despite dating a string of handsome young men, so far, a long-term, loving relationship had eluded her. Was she about to obtain such a relationship?

5

SHAW THING

You might well have seen Jason Shaw already in one of his high-profile advertisements for Tommy Hilfiger. After all, those posters, featuring Shaw in just his underwear, were difficult to miss. Women across the planet dreamed of getting to see a bit more of Shaw. Well, for Paris that dream came true.

Born in November 1973 in a conservative suburb of Chicago, Illinois, Shaw is one of the highest-paid male models of the modern era. His father John C. Shaw Jr is former President and Co-CEO of Jefferies & Co. Jason went to the University of Chicago to study history and had plans to start his own business once he graduated. However, through his college roommate, who was trying to get into modelling himself, Shaw entered a ProScout event in Chicago and was selected as the only male model from the many entrants. With this encouragement under his belt, he went to Manhattan and signed with Wilhelmina Models. Abercrombie & Fitch quickly offered him his first assignment and his career took off from there.

In his first two years as a model, Shaw got work from a host of big names including Tommy Hilfiger, Calvin Klein, DKNY, Gianni Versace, Lacoste, Gap, Karl Lagerfield fragrances, Ralph Lauren and many others. He appeared on catwalks around the world including in Milan, Paris and New York. Once he signed up exclusively with Tommy Hilfiger, he became a familiar face – and backside – on billboards across the USA.

It is highly likely, therefore, that Paris had already admired Shaw's talent before she first met him at a New York fashion party. The two were introduced by Patrick McMullan, the city's premier paparazzo. But it was not until six months later that they got it together, after bumping into each other at the L'Hermitage store in Los Angeles where Paris was picking an outfit for Oscars night. 'It was love at first sight,' says Shaw, somewhat inaccurately as he had already met her once. 'I saw this beautiful girl and I was overwhelmed. But I'm so shy. Luckily, Paris is not.' She wasn't shy in approaching him, nor in praising him. 'He's, like, the most beautiful man in the world,' she beamed to reporters. 'And he's so kind. The age difference is really good for us – he's 29, I'm 21. He teaches me a lot about history.'

The fact that Shaw was in a very lucrative trade made it easier for Paris to trust that he was not after her for her money. 'I make a very nice living,' he says, 'so it's not like, Oh, I'm scoring some rich girl. If her name was Smith and not Hilton, it would be fine.' Paris added, 'Happiness is love, not fame, not money. That's what I believe now.' She wrote in *Confessions* that she is good at spotting men who are just after her for her money. 'If he talks too much about how you're rich, and brings up money all the time, I can tell he likes money more than he likes me,' she writes. 'I think girls are gold diggers more often than guys, though. I haven't met too many guys who were out for my money. I think when it comes to girls, guys are motivated more by attraction than money. At least at my age.'

What fun the pair had. In July 2001, they attended a bonfire and disco held at the Hamptons estate owned by Louise MacBain, the CEO of the trader.com Website. The party was to celebrate the first screening of Disney's *The Princess Diaries*. Within weeks, Shaw was a guest at the Hilton residence in Southampton. The couple were seen looking loved-up at the Bow Wow Brazil benefit for the Animal Rescue Fund. They were also in romantic mood at a birthday party for Paris's dad, where Paris's mum sang karaoke. Also in attendance at that bash were billionaire David Koch, Olympian Bruce Jenner, and OJ Simpson murder case witness Faye Resnick.

Soon after this, a friend of Paris announced at a nightclub that Paris and Shaw had got engaged. The announcement was greeted with cheering and applause. But was it true? 'This whole engagement thing is a little awkward for me,'

Shaw told reporters. 'I love Paris and I want to be with her forever, but when I do it, I want it to be special. So to set the record straight, we are not engaged.'

'Not officially,' Hilton added. 'There's no ring, but we have these dog-tag necklaces that we wear all the time to show we belong to each other.' Aunt Kyle also denied the rumours. 'It's not true. They are very much in love, but there are no plans for marriage as of yet.'

In October that year, they were seen hand-in-hand at Tommy Hilfiger's party at the Hudson Hotel thrown to celebrate psychic Judith Turner's new book. Then, during a shopping expedition at ABC Carpet and Home, Paris was overheard affectionately calling Shaw 'Bitch'. In January of the following year, the couple looked very much in love at *Talk* magazine's Golden Globes party in LA, and a few months later, they were dancing the night away at media mogul Jason Binn's birthday party. Then it was on to a plane to attend the launch of the new Tommy Hilfiger store in Dusseldorf, Germany.

When they attended David Copperfield's 46th birthday bash, Paris was asked what she thought of magicians. 'David Blaine levitating is phat!' she grinned. A friend was on hand to quietly remind her that this party was for Blaine's rival, Copperfield. 'Oh, yeah. David Copperfield is cool, too,' she giggled. Asked if she had ever performed a magic trick, she said, 'I can make McDonald's French fries disappear! And I made Jason fall in love with me. We're not engaged yet, but we will be soon.'

Despite these public appearances, Paris preferred to

keep to quiet nights in with Shaw. 'Now I'm older my life is so different,' she said. 'Jason and I stay at home, watch DVDs. I've grown up a lot. In five years' time, I'll definitely be settled down, married with kids. Jason and I aren't engaged, but I'll definitely be with him forever.'

But she was not to stay with him forever. Admitting that she sometimes falls in love too fast – 'I know. It's always getting me into trouble' – she decided that they had to split. 'Unfortunately, it became clear we were at different places in our lives, but I'm hopeful we can remain friends,' she said. It was an upsetting time for Paris, who had never experienced such a serious relationship before. Her heartbreak was noticed by her family, too. 'Jason was her first love, her first serious relationship and it was hard for him to be in the spotlight,' her aunt Kyle says.

A journalist from the *Village Voice* newspaper recalls, 'They'd spent a lot of time apart. Paris's celebrity got bigger and bigger and it just got to big for him to handle any more.' They did remain friends and were often seen together after the split. 'He's still in love with her,' said a friend of Shaw.

There has always been and always will be interest in what Paris wears. However, a simple thin red string bracelet around her wrist attracted more coverage and comment than many of her most fashionable outfits. This string symbolised her interest in Kabbalah, the main form of Jewish mystic tradition. This branch of Judaism is more than 4,000 years old. It consists of a large body of speculation on the nature of divinity, and also includes many meditative, devotional, mystical and magical practices. These were only shown to a select few, leading it to become regarded as an esoteric offshoot of Judaism. Kabbalah has more than 3.5 million followers including an increasing number of celebrities including Madonna, David and Victoria Beckham, Britney Spears, Michael Jackson, Sarah Jessica Parker, Jerry Hall, Roseanne Barr, Caprice and Melinda Messenger.

The red string bracelets are said, by the Kabbalah movement to 'protect us from the influences of the Evil Eye. Evil Eye is a very powerful negative force. It refers to the unfriendly stare and unkind glances we sometimes get from people around us.' When asked why she was wearing one, Paris said, 'It helps you confront your fears. Like if a girl borrowed my clothes and never gave them back I would confront her. Just wearing the red string really keeps away bad energy and bad people in my life.' In a class about the Kabbalah, an eyewitness reported a funny incident involving Paris. 'People usually talk about relatives who have passed on, but Paris blurted out a story about a hot man. Nobody knew what to say.' How about: That's hot!?

6

VIDEO NASTY

Paris first met Rick Salomon in 2000, through a friend of a friend. He remembers that they took one look at each other 'and there it was, we hooked up right away'. Not that this came as a surprise to Salomon who says that he always falls in love fast and brags that he 'normally gets girls within 10 hours of meeting them'. Born in a blue-collar New Jersey town in 1968, Salomon is the son of a former executive vice-president at Warner Bros and grew up in luxury. However, his mother died when he was just 12 and his father, Salomon says 'was constantly working'.

When he was 15, he took off to Hollywood and attempted to get in on tinsel town's inner circle. He succeeded, thanks in part to his drug dealing. 'In my teens, I dealt in drugs big time,' he remembers. 'I became a carrier, taking kilos of this stuff, by air, from Los

Angeles to Miami and New York, and selling it on the streets. When I was 16, I was clearing $20,000 to $30,000 a month. In cash. I partied like there was no tomorrow. I thought I'd found paradise. I was a good-looking kid, I had all the girls chasing after me and I had dough in my pocket.'

So Salomon had many of the things you need to go places in Hollywood. The only thing he lacked was talent, so he kept hooking up with famous faces to try and shine in their reflected glory. His first wife was voice actress Elizabeth Daily, who was the voice behind many characters including Tommy Pickles in *Rugrats*, Buttercup in *The Powerpuff Girls* and the title pig in *Babe: Pig In The City*. The pair had two children during their five-year marriage.

After that marriage ended, Salomon married *Beverly Hills 90210* actress Shannen Doherty. It was a brief marriage. After nine turbulent months during which Salomon was reported to have had a string of affairs, the couple broke up. At various points in his life, Salomon is reported to have had flings with actress Drew Barrymore, supermodel Devon Aoki and Playboy playmate Nicole Lenz. However, his most publicised relationship to date was the one he had with Paris. Little could Paris have known when she first met Salomon what a profound and unpleasant effect he would have on her life. When the resultant controversy had died down, Paris was asked how the affair had changed her. 'Just not trusting people, knowing there's bad people in the world,' she replied.

Salomon says it was well known that he made video recordings of his sexual encounters and that Paris would have been aware of this when she met him. Whether she knew this from the start or not, she was certainly aware of his penchant for recording lovemaking by May 2001 when the couple taped themselves having sex. The resulting footage begins with a 19-year-old Paris playfully posing in front of the bathroom mirror, showing off her breasts. Then follows some of the video's few moments of genuine dialogue:

Rick: 'Let me see the pussy.'
Paris: 'Eeeeugh! I hate that word.'
Rick: 'What d'you want me to call it? Let me see your c*nt.'
Paris: 'Eeeeugh! Say, "I love you."'
Rick: 'I love you and can I please take off your pants. I love you and want to suck your pussy.'
Paris: 'No, say you love me and you want to kiss me.'

Much of the actual lovemaking scenes are shot in grainy night vision. At one point Paris interrupts the lovemaking to answer her phone. Paris says, 'Wait. Let me get my phone.' An annoyed Salomon responds, 'Yo, f*ck your phone!' As well as the sex scenes, the video also includes footage of the couple on a plane and at a swimming pool in a holiday resort.

Three years after these scenes were recorded, some of the footage surfaced on the Internet. The clip quickly pinged around computer screens across the world. It became the talk not of the town but of the whole globe. The media loved the story. All other issues were quickly forgotten, including for some the war in Iraq, which was less than two months old at this point. It wasn't just the gossip pages of the tabloids that covered the story; even the *New York Times* went big on it. The *New York Observer*, meanwhile, gave the tape a tongue-in-cheek review, saying, 'In her debut as an adult-film actress, Paris Hilton offers a good taste of things to come.'

As for Paris, she was devastated by this terrible invasion of her privacy and by the media's obsession with the story. As the story broke, she had been about to return to the US from Australia where she had been promoting the forthcoming series of *The Simple Life*. Paris and her family needed someone to manage the aftermath of the scandal and the man they turned to was Dan Klores. Head of DKC, one of the largest public relations firms in the world, Klores had previously helped Mike Tyson, Michael Jackson and Donald Trump out of sticky moments. Klores, who has been described as a 'pit bull', was based in Park Avenue and quickly got to work trying to help the Hiltons salvage something from the affair.

He described the whole affair as a storm in a teacup, and his strategy was informed by this. He decided not to force Paris to give a series of 'I'm so upset' interviews to the press. Quite the contrary, he ordered her to stay out of the public eye. Meanwhile, he attempted to assuage the appetites of the press himself by feeding quotes to hungry

Above left: Paris's great-grandfather, Conrad Hilton, the founder of the Hilton hotel chain.

Above right: The Waldorf-Astoria hotel in the 1980s. When they moved to New York it was here that they took up residency.

Below left: Her parents, Richard 'Rick' and Kathy Hilton.

Below right: Her younger sister Nicky.

Paris has taken the modelling world by storm, forging a successful career.

Above left: At the PlayStation Portable celebrity fashion show, New York, September 2005.

Above right: The 2 Be Free fashion show modelling the 2006 Spring–Summer collection, Los Angeles, October 2005.

Below left: Modelling for the prestigious designer Julien MacDonald. Here Paris is at London fashion week, February 2006.

Below right: At the Heatherette show for Spring–Summer 2007 collection, Olympus fashion week, New York, September 2006.

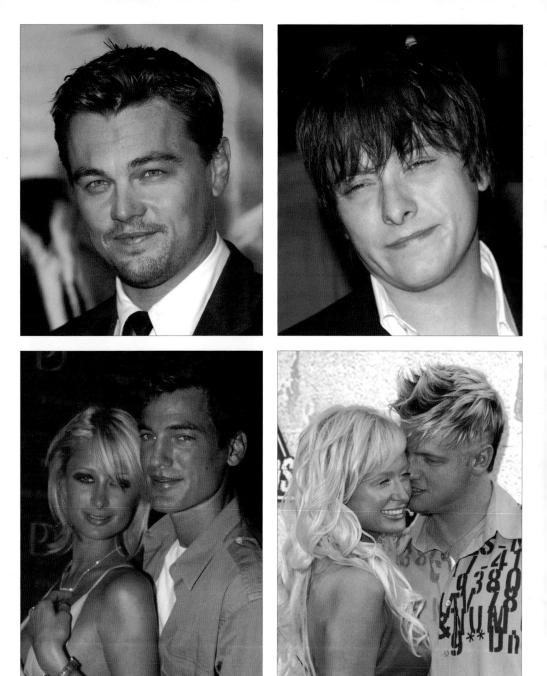

Paris's colourful love life has often been in the spotlight.

Above left: Her liaison with heart-throb Leonardo DiCaprio in 2000 was her first mention in a gossip column.

Above right: Edward Furlong, who she was linked to after splitting with DiCaprio.

Below left: With her first love Jason Shaw at Sean 'P Diddy' Combs' party for his album *P Diddy and the Bad Boy Family*, New York, September 2001

Below right: With Nick Carter at the MTV awards, June 2004.

In December 2003 *The Simple Life* reality television show launched Paris onto small screens around the world. Paris and best friend Nicole Richie were stripped of their luxuries and sent to stay on a farm with a family in rural Arkansas, USA.

Above left: Promotional shots of the show.

Above right: The Leding family with whom they stayed; (*left to right*) Richard, Curly, Janet, Braxton, Albert, Cayne and Justin.

Below: Hard at work on the farm.

To celebrate her 21st birthday Paris hosted 5 parties in 5 cities.

Above: Paris's first party at Studio 54 in New York, February 2002.

Below left: With Lady Victoria Hervey at the London leg of the celebrations. It was held at The Stork Rooms, May 2002.

Below right: Celebrity guests interior designer Nicky Haslam and Cilla Black.

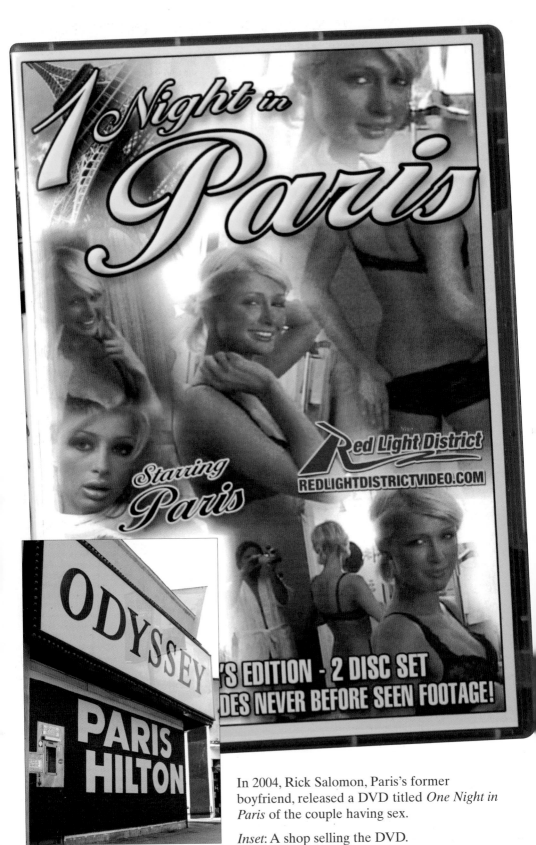

In 2004, Rick Salomon, Paris's former boyfriend, released a DVD titled *One Night in Paris* of the couple having sex.

Inset: A shop selling the DVD.

The summer of 2004 saw *The Simple Life* return for a second series. The girls travelled in a pink truck and Airstream Trailer *(above)* from Miami to Beverly Hills in a cross-country road trip. They were required to undertake several jobs that included getting deputised *(below left)* and catching crawfish *(below right)*.

In 2004 Paris published her book *Confessions Of An Heiress – A Tongue-In-Chic Peek Behind The Pose*. Among her insights she lists 23 instructions on 'How To Be An Heiress' and also '12 Things An Heiress Would Never Do'.

reporters. He told the *New York Observer*, that the footage was 'inconsequential to everything that's going on in the world and not really even interesting sex'. He added, 'It seems like a particularly dour time in our culture. There will be outlets that want to keep it alive.' While Paris hid, he continued to play the whole saga down.

Klores then felt it was time for Paris to make her first public statement on the saga. 'I feel embarrassed and humiliated, especially because my parents and the people who love me have been hurt,' began her written statement. 'I was in an intimate relationship and never, ever thought these things would become public.' Next on the agenda of Klores's strategy was the wheeling out of Paris's father Rick to give his support to his devastated daughter. 'I love my daughter,' he said. 'It goes without saying that I was severely unhappy when I heard about this tape. I will, however, do everything I can to support my daughter in every way possible.'

However, behind the scenes things were not entirely calm in the Hilton household. Her mother Kathy remembers, 'When it happened, I think I yelled at her, "If you're going to do something like that with a boy, then make sure you hide the damn thing." It was like a big wave coming over me. It was heartbreaking.' She sought the help of a therapist. Rick says, 'As a father, obviously it was quite upsetting. It was probably one of the most stressful things we've had to deal with as a family. It could have destroyed us, but it brought us closer together.'

Perhaps the sharpest move by Klores was booking Paris

on to *Saturday Night Live*, a late night American comedy-variety show based in New York City which has been broadcast live by NBC on Saturday nights since 11 October 1975. On the show she did a funny sketch with presenter Jimmy Fallon. Broadcast on 6 December 2003, the sketch ran like this:

Fallon: Is it hard to get into the Paris Hilton?

Paris: Actually, it's a very exclusive hotel, no matter what you've heard.

Fallon: Do they allow double occupancy at the Paris Hilton?

Paris: No!

Fallon: Is the Paris Hilton roomy?

Paris: It might be for you, but most people find it very comfortable.

Fallon: I'm a VIP. I may need to go in the back entrance.

Paris: It doesn't matter who you are. It's not gonna happen.

'It was a risk,' admits Klores of his media strategy for Paris. 'I shut down everything she was doing. I shut down everything the Fox people – her own network – were doing with her. I said, "I'll take the hit for this." I like being in the fight. From the start the only thing I was gonna let her do was *Saturday Night Live*. Her father said, "You're the only one she listens to." She was scared of me, which is what I wanted. But she was very disciplined; she came to

New York, didn't go anywhere and stayed in. She's a child. She may be 23, but she's a young 23.'

Paris's mother says the whole episode 'was handled with great dignity and grace. I think in life we are all dealt a deck of cards and we are a very supportive family and I thought it was handled very well.'

With the initial media frenzy at least somewhat abated, it was time to try and discover how the footage came to be public. The fingers were inevitably pointed at Salomon early on. He responded by initially denying that it was even him on the tape. Then his defence evolved into saying that yes it was him on the tape but that his roommate Don Thrasher had stolen the tape and sold it to a Seattle porn company. This was like a 'yeah but no but' defence years before *Little Britain* and Vicky Pollard ever hit our television screens.

When the Hilton family issued a joint statement about the scandal, certain clauses in it gave Salomon cause for concern. 'The Hilton family is greatly saddened at how low human beings will stoop to exploit their daughter Paris, who is sweet-natured, for their own self-promotion as well as profit motives. Paris is working very hard on her career. The release of a private tape between a younger girl and an older boyfriend is more than upsetting. Anyone in any way involved in this video is guilty of criminal activity, and will be vigorously prosecuted.'

Meanwhile, someone from the Hilton camp seemed to be implying that Salomon might have drugged Paris. This encouraged Salomon to take a more offensive line.

In November 2003, he filed a slander suit against the Hilton family for $10 million at Los Angeles Superior Court. In it, he insisted that Paris was an 'active participant' in making the video, but that she and her family had waged a 'cold, calculated and malicious campaign to portray Salomon as a rapist' to protect her image. He also made a $10 million claim against Marvad Corporation, the Internet company who were selling the tape, for invasion of privacy. After this, Marvad took out a writ against Don Thrasher.

As the suits flew back and forth, any sympathy that the public might have felt for Salomon was destroyed by his decision to start selling the tape himself. All his protestations that he had been embarrassed and hurt by the episode seemed false in the light of his link up with Red Light District Video. He called the video *1 Night In Paris* and tastelessly dedicated it to the memory of the victims of the September 11 attacks. He has reportedly made millions of dollars from this but he remains defiant. 'In this town it is dog-eat-dog,' he says shrugging. 'I figured that as everyone thought I'd released the tape anyway, I may as well go ahead and put my full-length version out there.'

'Paris, who's great grist for the mill, is in a tricky spot now,' said VH1's Michael Hirschorn. 'The thing about Pamela Anderson is that she was already an icon, with a pretty good sense of humour about her porn video with Tommy Lee. You're never really sure whether Paris gets the joke or not. She has succeeded in part because she's so inscrutable. But is she the Nietzschean über-babe who doesn't give a shit, or what? How does her personality fill out going forward?' As for Pamela Anderson herself, when she was asked what she thought of the video, her reply was simple: 'She should have kept her shoes on'.

As for Paris, it is only in the years after the scandal that she has found the strength to discuss it publicly. 'Someone sent it to me and I was, like, crying, I was so embarrassed,' she says. 'It was humiliating. I used to think it was so bad but it's like, everyone has sex. I'm sure everyone has filmed a tape. It's not like it was some random person. I was in love with that man. I was with him for three and a half years. We were together. I don't even really remember filming it, I was so out of it in that tape.'

She goes on to add, 'I was in an intimate relationship, never thinking that my foolish actions would become public. I can't walk the streets and don't want to go out any more. I don't want to party.' She says her parents were naturally 'heartbroken and humiliated' by the episode. However, there were no recriminations from them against their daughter. 'Well, they know I didn't do anything wrong,' she says. Asked how she feels now about Salomon, she says, 'He's a pig, he's disgusting. I really loved him and I was a stupid little girl. So I've learned a lot from my mistakes. He is making so much money. It makes me so mad. We were suing in the beginning but everyone has already seen it. Let him do whatever he wants. I don't want to go to court. He will fight me. I just want to get on with my life.'

Naturally, the episode continues to be raised whenever Paris is interviewed, which means she cannot completely leave it in the past. In 2005, in her cover interview for *Vanity Fair*, she spoke again of how she felt at the time. 'I'm like, great, thanks for wrecking my whole thing. I just worked so hard. I have my first TV show coming out, and I'm finally going to do something with my life and now everyone in the world will see me naked. My agent, everyone, was so scared. I think I handled it right and didn't do anything.'

There have been suggestions that part of Paris's settlement with Salomon is that she receives a royalty from every copy of *1 Night In Paris* that is sold. It would be a neat arrangement but she denies that this is the case. 'I didn't receive one dollar,' she insists. 'I've never received any money from it, ever. I was going to sue, but that meant I'd be in court for a whole year, spending millions of dollars. So I said, "I've just got to take this as a lesson in life. Don't ever trust anyone again like that, move on, and just forget about it." And I've forgotten about it, become a stronger person...' What her great-grandfather would have made of the original scandal cannot be known, but it's safe to assume he'd approve of the way she learned from it.

In April 2004, Salomon dropped his suit against the Hiltons, and Paris could indeed move on and forget about it. However, three years later, a similar scandal broke and she was once again forced to endure having her dirty linen viewed in public. Donald Trump admired how Paris fought on after the Salomon scandal. 'I hate what happened with that sex tape but it only made her hotter. She left that sleazebag so far behind that his head is spinning. He wouldn't even have a shot at her now.' Paris's final word on the episode, for now, shows how her faith helped her through it. 'It sucks. It's a horrible invasion of privacy. I cry and ask, why is this happening to me? But then, for some reason, I feel like I'm a good person, and God always helps me out. It could be so horrible for someone, but God always makes it turn around for me, I feel.'

In actioning that 'turning it around', Paris took to Australia to watch the Melbourne Cup. There she met a contestant from the nation's recent *Australian Idol* television contest, Robert Mills. The pair met at the premiere of *The Matrix Revolutions* in Sydney and spent that night together in a Sydney hotel. It must have been a steamy night because guests in the suite below the hotel spa complained that water from the spa kept dripping through their ceiling. Paris was rather coy when asked about Mills. 'I think he's just a nice, charming guy,' she smiled. Mills, too, was rather non-committal. 'Who's that?' he replied when asked about Paris. Pressed again, he gave a polite 'No comment.' The couple spent much of the Melbourne Cup day in the L'Oréal tent, smooching away.

She then took part in Wayne Cooper's autumn/winter collection show in Melbourne at Australian Fashion Week. Her first outfit made her appear like a naughty schoolgirl; she then appeared in a low cut black mini, a ruffled party dress and a glamorous black full-length gown. However, the real triumph for Paris was that Australia's own supermodel, Alyssa Sutherland, was relegated to second-billing in the show in favour of Paris.

Speaking of fashion, after three years with T Management, in 2002 Paris signed for Ford Models. Neil Hamil of Ford said his decision to sign her was very easy. 'I just fell in love with her. She's adorable. So I signed her.' It was a similarly straightforward process when Paris signed up to Guess. The co-founder and co-CEO of Guess, Paul Marciano, met her in the lobby of the Beverly Hills Hotel and Paris blew him away with her obsessive knowledge of the Guess label. 'She knew basically every campaign in the history of Guess,' he beamed. They agreed the details of a deal there and then. She appeared in three worldwide campaigns for Guess but quickly outgrew the label as her rising stardom made her increasingly busy.

'To even schedule to talk to her was becoming impossible,' said Marciano. 'This is where I realised she had become too big for Guess. But she definitely raised brand awareness tremendously around the world, instantly. People are obsessed with her like they were with Claudia Schiffer and Anna Nicole Smith, which is very unusual. It happens about every 10 years.'

Mills had been nowhere to be seen during the Wayne Cooper show and sure enough, the romance turned out to be just of the holiday variety. He confirmed this when he told an interviewer who asked about Paris, 'We're still in touch via email. And before you ask, no I don't have plans to go to the States. She's busy and I'm busy but I think I'm busier than her.' The pair spoke on the phone a few years later when Paris was in Australia to shoot *House Of Wax* but otherwise, that was that.

Mills made his name through reality television and producers of Australia's *Big Brother* show approached Paris while she was in the country. They wanted her to enter the *Big Brother* house as one of their 'put the cat among the pigeons' late entrants. Paris was tempted to see what the men in the house looked like but ended up replying with a polite 'no thanks', as did her sister Nicky when they subsequently asked her.

'It was really annoying in Australia with the press, the paparazzi,' Paris said. Paparazzi rented blocks opposite her hotel room and trained their lenses on her day and night. 'So, every time I'd be in, like, the hot tub or whatever, like, the next day it would be on the cover of every magazine,' Hilton said.

The media glare was as unrelenting as ever for Paris. However, having already been the focus of the paparazzi lenses and the big-screen movie-camera lenses, Paris was now ready to appear with her full consent in front of a different type of camera. The television variety.

7

THE SIMPLE LIFE

Brad Johnson, who worked in Fox Television's comedy department, was set a new challenge in 2002 – go and find a new way to produce funny television shows that broke away from the traditional sitcom format. 'The areas that seemed simplest and cleanest was to go back to those high-concept sixties sitcoms and say let's do them for real,' he remembers.

To this end, he returned to *Green Acres*, a sitcom first aired on CBS in the 1960s. In the show, New York lawyer Oliver Wendell Douglas – played by Eddie Albert – decides to leave the ratrace of Manhattan to live out his dream of being a farmer in the peace and tranquillity of the countryside. However, his socialite Hungarian wife Lisa – played by Eva Gabor – is not so chuffed about leaving the metropolis. The result is a hilarious series, as the couple struggle to adjust to life in the rural world.

Johnson felt that a reality show that took up the theme of rich socialites being moved to the middle of nowhere would be a hit, but at first he struggled to decide who to cast in such a show. Then he found out that the casting department at Fox had recently had a meeting with Paris. Sharon Klein, senior vice-president of casting at the studio, said she was quickly impressed by Paris. 'I'm used to meeting with actors who are putting on a facade,' Ms. Klein said. 'She was so real. She was funny. At that first meeting she did not come off as stupid. She was in her own reality and not embarrassed to talk about it. There was a sweetness to her.'

Everyone at Fox quickly agreed that Paris was just the person they needed for their new project. 'They wanted to see stilettos in cow shit,' is how one Fox employee remembers it. There was excitement right to the very top of the company. 'We waited for the right opportunity, and this one feels like a great entry into an arena that we're looking forward to dipping our toes into,' said Dana Walden, 20th Century Fox TV president.

Paris initially had her doubts about taking part. Her mother warned her that the programme makers were in all likelihood aiming to make fun of her. But Paris remembers that the producers begged her. 'Even to an heiress, that's fairly flattering. Particularly to an heiress.' She decided to go for it and this was probably one of the best decisions she ever made.

Paris was quick to announce her part in the show and it seems that initially it was only going to be her that was involved. 'I'm going to be living on a farm, kind of like the *Green Acres*, but it will just be me and my own show.' Of course, it turned out not to be just Paris in the show – Nicole Richie joined her. However, Fox's original target to be Paris's sidekick in the show was her sister. Nicky, though, was not keen on the idea and Paris for one thinks she was right to turn it down. 'She couldn't live the simple life, she wouldn't have lasted. No way.' As Richard Johnson of the *New York Post* observed, 'Nicky is much more reserved and cerebral than Paris. She doesn't like the spotlight as much as her sister does.'

The search for a replacement reportedly saw Paris consult her friends Bijou Phillips and Kimberly Stewart, and the search ended with Nicole Richie. The pair were asked whether they thought viewers would be laughing with them or at them. 'I really don't care,' shrugged Paris. 'Hopefully, they'll be laughing with us,' Nicole said. 'But if not, they'll be laughing anyway.'

So with the line-up finalized, it was time to send the girls to their new home for the filming. Where would that new home be? Paris didn't have a clue until the last moment. 'We didn't know where,' she says. 'We just knew it was a small town. We had no idea of what state or anything.' That small town was Altus, Arkansas. One of America's southern states, Arkansas has plenty of small towns in its midst and Altus is one of the smallest – just 817 people lived there at the most recent census to take place before the filming. It is best known for its wineries.

The family chosen to host Paris and Nicole were the

Leding family, who lived on a farm in Altus. Albert and Janet Leding had four children, Ryan, Justin, Cayne and Braxton. When Fox first called to ask them to be one of five families shortlisted from Altus as potential hosts for the show, the family's mother Janet was not keen at all. 'We thought it was going to be like a documentary, with sort of like exchange students,' she remembers, and she immediately gave the whole idea the thumbs-down. However, someone must have changed her mind because within a week, the crew were at her house shaping it up for use in the show. She also spoke to both girls' mothers. We didn't know a whole lot about Paris and Nicole,' says Albert. 'All I knew was that Nicole's father was Lionel Richie,' added Janet.

For the show Paris and Nicole had to leave behind their mobile phones, credit cards and all other luxuries and stay with the family in Altus. When they arrived, their clothing and entourage of luggage raised eyebrows among the Ledings. 'Well, their clothing is a little different from what most girls wear around here,' says grandma Curly. 'The way they were dressed scandalised people,' said pub owner Dan McMillan. 'That's just how we dress,' replied Paris. We don't have, like, farm clothes.'

There had already been plenty of drama and comedy before this. A farewell bash for the girls saw them arrive by helicopter to the approval of their friends and family. Then they got into a private jet that would take them to their still-unknown destination. 'Wouldn't it be cool if they took us to Paris,' said Nicole. Instead they arrived in

Arkansas and were shown a pick-up truck that they must drive to their final destination. 'This is so ghetto,' moaned Paris as she attempted to get the truck to work.

As they are shown around the Leding home, the girls are stunned to discover that there is only one bathroom for what will be nine residents during their stay. This had been an important factor for the programme makers. 'They had one bathroom,' said Gail Berman, president of Fox Entertainment. 'We thought nine people, one bathroom — Paris and Nicole coming into that house has to be funny.'

The girls are sent out to do some grocery shopping for the Ledings. On the list is pigs' feet. Paris asks Nicole: 'Who the hell eats pigs' feet? Eeew. Barf. Feet sounds bad enough. Pigs' feet is worse.' Also on the list is 'Bottled water, generic.' Paris asks: 'What does "generic" mean?' They are only given $50 for the provisions but the bill comes to $65. Nicole asks the cashier: 'Can't we just have it?' and he replies: 'No, you can't just have it. This isn't a soup kitchen.'

Paris quietly asks Nicole: 'What does that mean, "soup kitchen"?'

When they return to the house they are asked to help prepare dinner, which includes plucking chickens. 'I'll show you how,' offers Curly. They outright refuse to do this. 'I'll vomit,' warns Paris. Over dinner, the conversation is awkward to say the least. 'I couldn't imagine living out here,' says Paris. 'I'd die.' Nicole asks the children if they 'hang out at Wal-Mart' and Paris asks,

'What is Wal-Mart?' to dropped jaws around the table. 'Do they, like, sell wall stuff?' It's one of the show's most memorable moments but Paris admits she was feigning ignorance for comic effect. 'I was joking,' she said. 'I just chose to say that. I love Wal-Mart. There was nowhere else to go. I love it. They have everything. It's cool.'

When they head to bed they find ticks in the beds. Creepy-crawlies are one of Paris's biggest phobias and there is a chorus of 'Ewws'. Before bedtime, Albert calls a meeting during which he tells the girls that they'll have to take part in household chores and that their curfew time is midnight. This comes as a bolt out of the blue for the girls but Nicole manages to smile and assure their hosts that they will be no trouble. 'We're nice girls, despite what you may have heard,' she grins.

Then they sit out on the porch with Justin, the Leding's teenage son. 'He's so sweet!' says Paris after Justin steps away to fetch his jacket. 'He's cute,' Nicole agrees, before adding after a pause, 'We should have a threesome with him. Let him have something.' The girls burst into hysterical laughter and the show comes to a hilarious ending.

The show was aired on 3 December 2003 and drew a fantastic 13 million viewers. It also received great write-ups in the American press. Linda Stasi in the *New York Post* was particularly enthralled. 'This not only must-see TV, but are-you-kidding?-I-wouldn't-miss-it-for-the-world TV,' she wrote. 'The contrast between two people who were raised without one moral value between them – and a real, live American family that works dawn to dusk – is absolutely riveting. Chairman Mao couldn't have come up with a more compelling indictment of the rich. I felt like moving to Cuba after watching it.'

The *Philadelphia Inquirer* was also buzzing: 'It's one of the funniest things to hit the airwaves since *I Love Lucy*, with our clueless heroines soaring, unintentionally, as postmodern versions of Lucy and Ethel... Leave it to others to comment on the meaning of all this. I'm too busy laughing my pants off.' The *Post Standard* said: *The Simple Life* wins hands-down as the best new reality series and best new comedy of the fall season. The *Chicago Tribune* raved: 'Consider it a spectacular success' while the *Sun-Sentinel* concluded: 'Hang on, *The Simple Life* is going to be a wild and funny ride.' The *Hollywood Reporter* simply added: 'There is almost no way *The Simple Life* can fail.'

Episode Two opened with the ominous statement: 'One of the cornerstones of *The Simple Life* is good old-fashioned work.' The girls are sent to work at a dairy farm. Arriving one hour late clad in bright-orange Von Dutch caps, they are told they will have to 'clock in' each morning. 'You ever clocked in anywhere before,' they are asked by the dairy farmer. 'You ever worked anywhere before?' They answer 'no' in unison to both questions.

Paris and Nicole's tasks include waking, herding and milking the cows, bottling the milk, washing the barn and filling up the troughs. 'I'm never going to drink milk again,' says Paris, 'now that I know where it comes from.' As they attempt to bottle the milk, lots gets spilled so they end up topping up the bottles with dirty water. Paris says: 'I feel sorry for the people who get them.' Nicole: 'Why? It'll be less fattening – I'm doing them a favour.' In the end, the hot tub in the garden seems a nicer option and the pair get into their bikinis and head out. When the farmer tries to get them back to work, Paris complains to the camera: 'He's so rude to us, he's treating us like animals.'

'I don't know exactly what it is you all are looking for in life,' he says as he fires them, 'but I hope you find it.' They thank him and leave with $42 pay for their troubles. That evening, there is a barbecue and the pair hope for a fun time with 'hot guys'. The atmosphere at the barbecue could scarcely be more tense. Instead, the girls head out to a local nightclub where, naturally, they go down a storm.

During the series they found themselves having to perform what were for them humiliating tasks but they manage to inject consistent hilarity into the proceedings. For instance, when they worked at the Sonic Burger fast-food restaurant, their tasks included cooking food, serving customers and taking out trash. They cheekily edited the marquee sign to 'Half Price Anal Salty Weiner Burgers', and were quickly fired.

They also found themselves having to perform a pregnancy test on a cow in a particularly icky moment. 'We had to put baby oil on a glove and shove my friend's hand up its ass,' remembers Paris with understandable distaste.

When they were sent to buy cow feed, they charged

some extra things to their employer's account including a full-length folding mirror and a birdhouse to give to Janet Leding for Mother's Day.

The girls then went on to work at a petrol station. This proves to be their favourite task to date, mainly because it gives them opportunities to check out the local boys. Nicole sets her sights on a boy called Anthony. However, Paris opts for Trae Lindley who was working at the Lakeside Food Mart. He was approached by Paris, who had clearly noted and fallen for his exceptional good looks. 'She told me, "Stay here and talk awhile," he remembers. 'I was too nervous at the time to remember what I was talking about. I couldn't even remember what was said after I was done talking to her.'

Paris asked him for his phone number and called him soon afterwards. 'We talked for two hours,' said Lindley. 'After that, it felt like we were really good friends. I was in shock for a little while, but after I got to know her, it felt really different. I didn't feel like she was so famous.

'People knew she had the hots for me and I had the hots for her. It was a lot of fun,' says Lindley. 'Paris is a lot different than what people make her out to look like. Many people make her out to be a dumb blonde, but she's a lot different.'

However, the constant intrusion soon got to him. 'I got tired of the cameras, and I know how she feels because they're all over the place,' he says. 'There were times when they left her alone, but they were there – in our face – most of the time. They'd hear every little whisper.'

Those who saw the pair together agreed that they seemed an adorable couple. 'They were really smitten with each other and if you saw them together, it was really cute,' says Shannon Burns, 39, a manager at Fat Tuesday. 'Seeing them out, it was more of an innocent, teenage-type relationship than what you see of her out-and-about.'

Paris met Trae's parents when she and Nicole had dinner with the family. 'They ate very little,' says dad George Lindley. 'But they were very well mannered. Paris was very nice, very sweet and not like she is portrayed in magazines.' Mother Tammy Lindley added, 'They were very normal when they came to dinner. They thanked us. They were very cordial.'

Nicole was far from cordial at the close of the series, when her purse was stolen at a bar and she threw bleach over a pool table in disgust. The series ends with her apologising to the bar owner and the pair heading off into the sunset, after promises to stay in touch with everyone they met in Altus.

Perhaps the biggest talking point of the series was whether Paris really is as dumb as she portrays herself to be on the show. 'I'm playing a character. I'm playing dumb. I'm kidding around,' she said on the *Late Show With David Letterman*. She later expanded on this theme. 'On the TV series I am playing a character, trying to be funny. I'm not like that in real life; I would never screw up all those jobs like that. I am doing it for the entertainment. I am just playing a role... I am sure some people think that

I'm like that, but imagine if we did all those jobs correctly. It wouldn't be funny. Everyone around us knows it's a TV show and everyone involved is in on it.'

The show finished its first American season with an average of 11 million viewers per night, finishing in the top third of the 100 most popular shows in the country. A second series was quickly commissioned and Paris's presence in it was seen as absolutely vital. 'The bottom line for Fox is that there's no TV show unless Paris is in it,' said an insider. 'So let's ask, what can Paris do? It's not like she's Josephine Baker, who could actually sing. It doesn't even matter what the TV show is about. Because she's now an internationally known strumpet, the guys who have seen the flailing and thrashing on the net will tune in. They're your 18 to 49 television demographic, and that's why there's a second season.' Back in the real world, meanwhile, Paris, as ever, believes in living the dream.

Sum 41 is a Canadian pop-punk band formed in 1996, 41 days into the summer – hence the peculiar name. Their heavy touring policy has helped them sell millions of albums and become a major band in their circle, with appearances on US TV shows like the *Late Show With David Letterman* and *Saturday Night Live*. Their lead singer, Deryck Whibley, is a hero to the short-trousered kids who follow the pop-punk scene and a pin-up to plenty of girls.

In April 2003, the *New York Post* first reported Paris's relationship with Whibley. She had been spotted smooching with him in a Hollywood hotspot. The Page Six story linked Paris's story with Kelly Osbourne, who was rumoured to be linked with a different member of Sum 41. 'Fresh from her break-up with Bert McCracken, singer for the Used, Osbourne is said to have a serious crush on Sum 41 bassist Cone McCaslin. Can it get any cuter?' asked the article. Well, it did get cuter two months later, when the same newspaper reported that another of Paris's friends was involved with a Sum 41 member. 'Paris's pal Nicole Richie is apparently getting in on the action as well, and has been hot and heavy with Sum 41 drummer Steve Jocz,' it claimed, alongside a report of Paris' and Whibley's antics at KROQ's Weenie Roast in Irvine and The Whiskey and Dolce afterwards. An eyewitness said Paris and Whibley 'were going at it like there was no tomorrow'.

Born in March 1980, Whibley is now best known for his marriage to singer Avril Lavigne. He has always had an eye for a celebrity squeeze. When asked by *Playboy* which celebrities he fancied he replied, 'That's a hard one, because there are a lot. I'd have to say Carmen Electra, and not just because I think she's hot. I've read interviews with her, and she seems like she's a really cool girl. Do you know her? Can you help me out here? Nah, I'm just kidding.'

During her relationship with Whibley, however, it was Paris who was linked with a celebrity female. In September 2003, she was rumoured to have been smooching with Ingrid Casares in Miami's South Beach.

Casares is best-known for her relationships with Sandra Bernhard and then Madonna. She is a huge figure on the Miami social circuit and very well connected in celebrity circles. However, Paris denies that she and Casares ever connected in that way. 'We were dancing but I never kissed her,' she swears. 'We're just friends. Besides, I was with my boyfriend the whole time.' Casares also denied the pair had got it on together. 'We danced together,' she insisted. 'We hung out all weekend.' Asked if their lips touched, she said, 'Just hello and goodbye.'

So shaken up was the Hilton camp by these reports that Paris's mum even emerged to lend her weight to the denials. 'The fabrication that Paris was romantically involved with Ingrid Casares is a desperate attempt to promote various businesses,' she said. 'I warned my girls that when you accept plane tickets and hotel accommodations, there is no such thing as a free lunch.'

But shortly after this, Paris, Whibley and Casares did the South Beach party rounds after the Latin Grammy awards. In the wake of the recent fevered speculation, their antics turned heads. 'Paris and Deryck looked all lovey-dovey,' said an eyewitness. 'But when Ingrid showed up, he started acting very jealous and steered them away from each other. Paris kept saying, 'No, I want to speak with Ingrid."' Later that night, another eyewitness reported, 'Paris and Deryk kept bickering. Finally, he whisked her out of the club. Ingrid was looking for them, but they'd already left. Casares reaffirmed that there was nothing between her and Paris.

If Whibley was the jealous sort, he would have had more fuel added to the fire when he read reports that suggested Paris and rock singer Mark McGrath had enjoyed a steamy session in the toilets at a television bash. A guest claimed, 'This girl came over and said, "Oh my God, the best hook-up in show business is happening right now in the bathroom." I couldn't believe it when Paris came out. She was so obvious about it.'

Paris strongly disputed the story, so much so that she phoned the newspaper that published it. 'Are you kidding? That's bull!' she told them. 'I'm in love with Deryck. I'm meeting him in London in, like, a week. Mark and I have been friends for, like, six years. And I wasn't in a bathroom with him. I was sitting with him by the pool ... I've never hooked up with him, and I never would.'

She also set aside some space in *Confessions* to straighten out the rumour. 'The rumours about me and Mark McGrath were complete lies ...We were both laughing about that, wondering where it came from. Mark's my friend. Contrary to everything you might think, I really prefer having one boyfriend. I'm friends with lots of guys, but I don't like dating unless I'm really into somebody.'

Nonetheless, her relationship with Whibley was soon over. After he and Paris split up, the rocker insisted he had no regrets. When asked about her sex video, Whibley quipped, 'I haven't seen it. I mean, I lived it – I don't need to see it!' He ended up with Avril Lavigne, prompting the *Sun* to quip that he 'swapped upper-crust for crusty.' Meow!

Speaking of meow, in 2003 Paris added another film to her CV with a small part in *The Cat In The Hat*. Starring Mike Myers, the film was based on a 1957 Dr Seuss cartoon book. The film drew criticism for the somewhat adult humour and content, one journalist complaining, 'I'm not sure the mild gags about gas-passing, cat pee, butt cracks and nose-picking would have won Seuss' affections. Would he have wanted a flash of Paris Hilton bumping and grinding?' Paris's part was a cameo only seconds long but it added to her prestige.

Her interest in and love of animals increased after she met Heather Mills McCartney at her then-husband Sir Paul's Beverly Hills home to watch a video exposing animal cruelty. Paris says, 'From that point on I've never worn fur and I never will. I haven't eaten any meat since. I just survive on pasta and stuff like that. I was grossed out. It was disgusting.'

She also appeared in a short film in 2003, *L.A. Knights*, playing Sadie who is – wait for it – a blonde heiress to a family fortune. A man breaks into her bank and suddenly her fortune is gone. Paris has to take a part-time job just to survive and also track down the man who stole her money. Written and directed by M. Eastling, it was a great addition to her CV and included her boyfriend Jason Shaw in its cast.

Shaw also starred alongside Paris in another indie film in 2004 – *The Hillz*. This is a film was described by one of its cast as *Boyz N The Hood* meets *Stand By Me*. The film centres around four affluent suburban teenagers who indulge in violence, drugs and casual sex. Amazon.com describes it as 'a comedic pulse-pounding adventure on the "hood's" leaf-strewn streets'. In the film, the lead character Steve, played by *Charmed*'s Jesse Woodrow, is the rival to Shaw's character for the affections of Heather, played by Paris.

Another of the cast, *Anger Management* star Silas Gaither, says of the film, 'It's a story about kids growing up in Beverly Hills, young, with the drugs and temptations, the money.' He enjoyed working alongside Paris. 'She is a sweetheart. I think people give her a hard time.'

In fairness, a lot of people gave the film a hard time, too. The *Fresno Bee* newspaper described it as 'The story about how the young and privileged find a distraction from boredom through acts of violence,' but the reviewer managed to heap abuse on it from thereon in. Online it had a harsh response too, though one reviewer did manage to find a positive in it. 'At least we get to see Paris Hilton in a bikini,' wrote one online critic. Another online reviewer wrote, 'Paris has a respectable role and does a fair job; the director uses her wisely. A very interesting and often amusing late-night rental.' One Internet enthusiast gushed, 'It's one of the most entertaining movies I'd ever seen and I've seen a lot! Paris is sexy sexy sexy in this movie.' Another added, *The Hillz* is a wonderful modern day drama from first time writer and director Saran Barnun. *The Hillz* features strong performances from young actors like Rene Heger, Jesse Woodrow and Jason Shaw. Even Paris Hilton does a good job playing "the unattainable" Heather. Definitely worth seeing.'

It debuted at the second annual Boston International Film Festival, and one of the organisers said their aim was to 'generate more hype around' the event. Good move to involve a Paris film then! During her promotional junket, Paris amused one interviewer who asked her about the film. 'I'm, like, really excited. This movie is about a group of us with loads of money, who kinda doss around,' she said. The journalist asked her if the film was therefore a case of art imitating life? 'You know maybe it could be,' she replied. 'I guess I have seen that side of life.' Despite the harsh reviews, the filmmakers were pleased with the venture and cited it as one of the reasons for an increase in their profits. *Image Entertainment* reported net income of $1.1 million in the May 31-end quarter, up from $973,000 million in the same period a year earlier. Exciting things were also happening to another member of the Hilton family that year...

In August 2004, Paris was in attendance as maid of honour as her sister Nicky got married to Todd Meister at a 3 am ceremony. The apparent spontaneity of the ceremony surprised many, not least the president of the chapel where they wed. 'They came in saying they wanted the best,' said Shirley Harvey, who had already wed 29 couples that day when Nicky and Meister called just before closing time. 'They seemed pleased and happy when they left.' Paris was the only other family member of the ceremony. 'It was a beautiful, small wedding with an amazing energy,' said Jeff Beacher, the Hard Rock Hotel entertainer who served as best man. 'The two of them are very much in love.' The wedding surprised many, but not friends of Meister. 'Todd will dance all night, he'll jump on a plane at the last minute and go anywhere to have a good time,' says Ginny Donahue, a long-time friend. 'I think Todd and Nicky share the same philosophy – live for the moment.'

So why did they marry, seemingly on a whim? 'They were planning on getting married this fall, but while in Las Vegas they felt there'd be less attention if they did it there,' explained her long-time publicist Elliot Mintz. 'They're happy and doing well. This is a real, meaningful, loving relationship. They are glowing.' Not that they had long to glow together, for the honeymoon was far from a lengthy affair. Nicky quickly flew to Cabo San Lucas, Mexico, for a *Maxim* photo shoot and her husband had to head back to New York for business meetings.

So who is Todd Meister? 'He's a long-time friend of the family,' said Couri Hay, a close friend of Nicky's parents, Kathy and Rick Hilton. He had been at Christmas and birthday celebrations with the family. 'I know that Kathy and Rick really like him,' added Hay. In 2001, he carried Nicky out of the Met Costume Gala, when it appeared she might have had a little too much to drink, but it was not until 2003 that the US press began to link them romantically. 'A family friend. He's the funniest person

I've ever met'. 'The wedding was 'planned,' she adds, telling Stuff, 'Paris orchestrated everything.'

Nikki Haskell, a long-time friend of Meister's, predicted a long and happy marriage for the pair. 'This is a perfect place to start. They are both young, attractive, sophisticated. They might have a real chance.' Sadly, though, the marriage was over as quickly as it was seemingly planned. In October, at an event for presidential hopeful John Kerry, it was noticed that Nicky wasn't wearing her diamond wedding ring. A reporter asked her whether she was still married and Nicky replied mysteriously, 'Am I?'

A Hilton family friend confirmed to the press that the marriage was over. 'They remain the best of friends, but she's 21, and it's just not the right time in her life for her to be married.' Meanwhile, a friend of Meister said that it was a difference in their levels of party stamina that did for them. 'It's really about their age difference. Todd loves to go out, but one's definition of partying at 33 is a helluva lot different than at 21.' Nicky then took up with Kevin Connolly, star of HBO's *Entourage* show. Her marriage to Meister had lasted just 21 days. Well, that's a lot longer than Britney Spears's 55-hour marriage to Jason Allen Alexander!

8

IT'S A DOG'S LIFE

There is some confusion about the origins of the Chihuahua breed. Some believe that these dogs arrived on the shores of America in 1519, with the Spanish armies of conquistador Hernando Cortes. Others say they arrived with the Chinese. Let the doggie historians argue it out between them, because there is no such controversy on the origins of possibly the world's most famous Chihuahua: Tinkerbell Hilton.

The Chihuahua is the ultimate toy lapdog. Although petite and fragile, it is very alert with a naturally bold nature. They are also very loyal dogs that make perfect companions. Their large eyes and erect ears make them irresistibly cute. Paris was unable to resist the allure of these adorable dogs and acquired Tinkerbell on 31 October 2002 from a dog-selling Website. Appropriately enough, the Chihuahua who was to enjoy a jet-set lifestyle arrived on a plane.

A Teacup Chihuahua, Tinkerbell weighs just two pounds and is known as 'Tink' to Paris who takes her little pet everywhere. Consequently, this tiny little dog has become a star in her own right. Tink has appeared on numerous red carpets and at a succession of celebrity parties. She has her own page on the Internet Movie Database, she has 'authored' her own book and was a star of *The Simple Life* series. Her fame is thought to have prompted an increase in sales of the breed.

To say Paris adores Tinkerbell would be an understatement. 'Tink is like my daughter,' purrs Paris. 'I know Tink and I are a lot alike, and Tink thinks a lot like me. She's a little princess, so cute and sweet.' And Paris dresses Tinkerbell like a princess. She has fitted her out in pink and white Fifi & Romeo coats, Chanel outfits and lots of designer shoes. 'Tinkerbell is the most fashionable dog in the world. Bambi (her other Chihuahua) will not wear clothes, though. I'll try to put them on, and he'll start biting and attacking me.' Next to her bed she keeps photographs of the animal.

It's almost like she's a proud parent, she certainly never misses a chance to talk about them. 'What's 'hot' right now?' Paris was once asked by an interviewer. This fashion queen could have dropped the names of any number of clothing lines. Instead she said, 'Well, my dog Tinkerbell is hot and I'm hot.'

In 2004, Tinkerbell put paw to paper and 'wrote' a book called *The Tinkerbell Hilton Diaries – My Life Tailing Paris Hilton*. As told to D. Resin, this is a fictional – though often eerily close to the truth – account of how it is to be the dog of a famous heiress. This is not the first time that a famous dog has 'written' a book. Barbara Bush's dog Millie wrote a bestselling view of the White House in the 1980s, and Bill Clinton's cat Socks gave its own perspective in 1993. However, neither title comes close to the biting satire of Tinkerbell's effort, which comes in the shape of a diary.

'Oh, for the love of God,' writes Tinkerbell in one entry, 'I'm in a pink angora sweater... I'm one of those dogs now, the kind that people cheer when a falcon swoops down and disappears into the sky with one in its talons... I just saw my reflection in the limo window – I look like the shit that a very flamboyant shark would take after it ate [fashion designer] Isaac Mizrahi.'

Her accounts of overhearing conversations involving Paris are always amusing. In one example, Tinkerbell overhears Paris telling a friend that she just watched the film *Gandhi*.

'If we really had people like that,' says Paris, 'Then, like, the world would be very different.' An eavesdropping Tinkerbell writes of her owner: 'She's almost cute sometimes.' The Chihuahua also predicts that one of Paris's deepest fears is 'The earth-killing giant asteroid scenario – there's just no way I can beat that thing for press coverage.'

It's a great light-hearted little read. Tinkerbell reports on Paris's jet-setting life and endless shopping expeditions, her encounter with the Dalai Lama on an aeroplane, and even jokes that Paris will cure cancer in our lifetime. We even have a dog's-eye view of the Rick Salomon video affair. Given how many dry digs Tinkerbell makes at Paris in the book – she moans that she has to 'smell heiress armpit all day long' – *The Tinkerbell Hilton Diaries* are once again proof of the sense of humour the heiress has. It is hard to imagine many of Paris's detractors authorising such mockery of themselves. 'I like how someone who can't work a toaster without causing a third-degree burn can engineer both continued solid tabloid coverage for the next month, and a for-certain mention and likely guest appearance on a popular national television show all in one fell swoop in under five minutes,' observes Tinkerbell.

The book was published in August 2004 and received glowing reviews, with the *Daily News* describing it as 'A Paris Tell-All With Bite', but shortly before publication, disaster struck when Tinkerbell suddenly vanished without a trace. Only days earlier, Paris's Hollywood Hills home had been broken into by someone who took jewellery and cash. For Paris, this was heartbreakingly upsetting. She immediately arranged to cover the neighbourhood with Missing posters, which read 'Please help. This dog is like a child to me.' Initially, Paris offered a $1,000 reward but quickly upped the stakes to $5,000.

To avoid an opportunist seeing to make a fortune from Paris's grief, the posters made no mention of Paris and did not name Tinkerbell. 'If they find out Tinkerbell is my dog, they'll hold it for ransom,' Paris explained.

'Everyone knows I'm rich, so they'll want millions.' However, news of Tinkerbell's disappearance soon leaked and naturally the media jumped all over the story. 'Ay, chihuahua! Paris is missing a pal', ran the headline in the *Daily News*. The accompanying story couldn't resist making a dig at Paris, even during this traumatic period for her. 'Let's hope Tinkerbell is found soon, before she does something crazy, like making a doggy-style video with some undesirable schnauzer.'

The *State* newspaper, meanwhile, speculated that the tale behind Tinkerbell's disappearance could be that Tinkerbell was 'dognapped' by an angry Taco Bell customer. As the story got bigger and bigger, *USA Today* wondered,

'Was Tinkerbell on a quest to liberate Shih Tzu Honey Child from the Nicole Richie compound?

'Did Tinkerbell check into a canine Betty Ford treatment centre? (Four days in dog years is equivalent to 28 human days.)

'Could Tinkerbell have flown the coop in a jealous rage, as the *New York Post* suggested? After years as an only pet, tiny Tink was recently joined by a Pomeranian named Prince, a ferret and a kitten.'

On 18 August, Paris announced that she and Tinkerbell had been reunited. Further details were not offered as to how Tinkerbell had been found or whether a reward was handed over. True to form, media cynics soon stamped all over the happy ending. One report suggested that the story behind Tinkerbell's disappearance was that Paris left the dog at her grandparents' home and simply forgot she'd done so. Other jealous swipers suggested that the whole story was made up to get free publicity for the publication of *The Tinkerbell Hilton Diaries*. Paris denies both suggestions.

'People want them as a fashion statement, and that's the wrong reason to get a Chihuahua or any other toy breed,' said Texan Lynnie Bunten, of San Antonio, Texas, who has bred the dogs for decades. 'They get tired. They get sensory overload. They can get dehydrated. A lot of Chihuahuas don't like strangers. Personally, I don't think Tinkerbell looks happy in the pictures I've seen. Tinkerbell looks stressed.' Not long after this, readers of two dog magazines voted Paris the worst celebrity dog owner. 'Our readers felt Ms Hilton's dog-parenting skills left a lot to be desired,' said Leslie Padgett, the editor of the two dog magazines. 'First she loses Tinkerbell, then she ditches her for a cuter dog, then replaces that dog with a ferret, then a kinkajou monkey and then, I gather, a goat.' She displayed some ignorance herself, there – the kinkajou is not a monkey.

It is easy for magazine readers to vote that Paris is a bad dog owner; none of them had ever met Paris or Tinkerbell. Those that do are full of praise for how well the heiress treats her dog. Perhaps the little dog was aware of all this media swiping for she later bit a television producer. 'Tinkerbell wasn't kidding – she really bit in good,' a witness said. 'The producer had to shake the dog off. It was a nasty bite.' Within weeks, the reunited dog and owner were spotted happily sauntering along at the Shore Club on Miami's South Beach. Tinkerbell was wearing a pink Chanel suit and looking the picture of health.

Paris revealed just how important Tinkerbell is to her when she explained how the dog even helps her choose boyfriends. 'Tink has a big say. If she likes a guy, I know they're good,' she said. 'I'd go out with a guy who was really funny and honest, or someone Tinkerbell really liked.'

When she travelled to Dublin to promote her perfume, Paris demanded five-star treatment not just for herself but also for Tinkerbell. She made sure that gourmet food was served for her dog in designer bowls. She also had groomers on hand to make sure Tinkerbell — who wears a diamond-studded collar — looked her best. When she promoted the perfume in London, Paris received a huge wet kiss from Tinkerbell in front of the assembled press.

'Tinkerbell watches herself on TV. She knows it's her and she knows my voice. And you can buy these DVDs called *Cat Sitter* and *Dog Sitter*. I got them both. All these cool things come on TV and the cat or dog will watch. If you're away, you can leave it on for the day and they love to see it.'

As well as Tinkerbell, Paris has had many other pets including three Pomeranian dogs, one of which is called Prince. She was asked whether the dogs get jealous of each other. 'All dogs are jealous,' she replied. 'They are like kids — kids would get jealous among themselves if you got a new kid. But I give them equal attention.' She has also had two ferrets, which she bought in Las Vegas, and a kitten. However, the pet that has come nearest to rivalling Tinkerbell in terms of column inches is Baby Luv, her aforementioned kinkajou.

Also known as Honey Bears, kinkajous are South American tree-dwelling mammals that weigh between 2 and 3 kilos. Nocturnal creatures, they dislike being awake during the day. If they become agitated, they may emit a scream and attack, usually clawing their victim and biting deeply. Some of those who have got on the wrong side of Paris in various nightclubs might say she has some characteristics in common with this animal. However, there the resemblance ends, because the shrill call of a kinkajou, which resembles a woman's scream, has led to them sometimes being called the 'crying woman' and plucky Paris doesn't like to cry.

However, in November 2005, she would have had to be extremely brave when her pet bit her while she was shopping for Agent Provocateur underwear. Many women have grown accustomed to their boyfriends being moody and bored while they are shopping for clothes, but few of those boyfriends will have bitten their girls. That's just what kinkajou did. All the same, Paris showed that she is a responsible and caring pet owner because she did not retaliate or dump her pet. The incident did get plenty of column inches, though, and was included in the *Daily Telegraph*'s end of year quiz.

The following year, Baby Luv attacked Paris again. She was frolicking with her exotic pet early one August morning 'the way some people play with their cats and dogs,' said her spokesperson, when Baby Luv bit her. 'It's a superficial bite on her left arm,' he added. Hilton was concerned that she was bleeding and went to hospital. 'She was seen by a doctor, who treated the wound, gave her a tetanus shot, cleaned the wound and applied something to it,' he concluded.

Baby Luv might have got her teeth out but an animal rights spokeswoman got her claws out when she said in the wake of the attack, 'It seems Paris thinks animals are as disposable as her friends and fiances,' said Lisa Lange of People for the Ethical Treatment of Animals (PETA). Not that any of this was enough to put Paris off her penchant for exotic pets. She told reporters that she was now thinking of getting a tiger. However, before she could realise this ambition, it transpired that kinkajous are restricted species in Los Angeles. Steve Martarano, spokesman for the California Department of Fish and Game said, 'We'll send them a letter just to let them know we're aware they have a restricted species.' Paris received defence from her people. 'She is a law-abiding citizen,' spokesman Elliot Mintz said. 'If she receives a letter from the Fish and Game people, I'm sure it will be reviewed and acted upon accordingly.'

Meanwhile, Paris was ready to take even further strides into the business world and she was going to surprise everyone with what a success she made of it.

9

MAKING SCENTS

I n May 2004, Paris took yet another step in refuting the 'famous for being famous' accusation that has been thrown at her for so long. She launched a fragrance range in conjunction with leading firm Parlux Fragrances, which has a variety of fragrances on its books including Perry Ellis, Guess and Ocean Pacific. Celebrity scents are all the rage now, as witnessed by ranges like Curious by Britney Spears, Daring by Isabella Rossellini, White Diamonds by Elizabeth Taylor, Belong by Celine Dion and Miami Glow by J. Lo.

Parlux shouted its deal with Paris from the rooftops. 'We're very excited to be working with Paris on this fragrance,' screamed Ilia Lekach, chairman and chief executive officer. It turns out that it was Lekach's son who put forward Paris as a possible name to chase. 'He's attuned to popular culture and thought Paris would be perfect for us,' Lekach said. 'He got me very excited about doing this deal. Paris has the right demographics for us, and she has both US and international appeal. Certainly, she has a great appeal among teenagers, but I think that most women admire her. She is very fashionable, and always at the right events and parties. She is very charismatic.'

With her global profile and her relentless ability to keep herself and her projects in the public eye, Paris was indeed an ideal person for Parlux to pin a product to. Added Lekach, 'Paris Hilton is a prominent part of our popular culture, with tremendous US and international following. We back all of our brands with strong advertising campaigns and plan to do print ads for this scent. But the beautiful thing about Paris is that she is so well known. She makes news wherever she goes. We also plan to hold major launch events when the fragrance is released.'

As for Paris, she was delighted with the deal. 'It's really hot. I mixed all these scents together… it smells so good. It's just something I've wanted to do since I was a little girl. I loved Barbie and Louis Vuitton, and I wanted to have my own brand.'

The official Website for the product described the scent in lavish terms: 'This fragrance opens with a sheer sophistication that personifies its creator, Paris Hilton. Chic enough to be worn on the catwalks of Milan while retaining a brilliant flirtatious charm, this head-turning fragrance can be dressed up or down for both day and evening wear.' Paris subsequently added a second fragrance called Just Me. 'It's definitely more mature,' she said of the new scent, which had floral touches, warmer sandalwoods and vanilla.

Her promotional tour for the perfume whipped up the usual level of excitement. In New York she appeared at Macy's Herald Square store on 34th Street. 'We bought the bottle so we could meet her,' said one excited fan who had also been given a limited edition Paris pass. Another fan called Michael Cresanti-Daknis turned up with a homemade poster that read: 'I Love You, Paris' and six red roses to give to her. He was asked why he liked her so much and replied, 'She's hot'. He was 10 years old. He wasn't able to deliver the roses in person. 'They told me they were going to give them to her later,' he shrugged.

Once Paris appeared in the main floor's beauty arcade, she brought the place to a standstill. Wearing an empire-line Diane von Furstenberg dress and Prada heels, she was dressed to kill. Everyone whipped out camera phones and snapped away. 'Buy my fragrance – it's sexy and hot and so are all of you!' she smiled during an appearance in California's Brea Mall. Moving on to Mexico on her promotion trail, she added that the fragrance smells like flowers and said, smiling, 'I love Mexico. The people are so nice.'

Nice, too, were the initial sales of her fragrance. In the third fiscal quarter of 2004, it generated $4.3 million in revenue and then made $6.7 million in the following quarter. Lekach was, naturally, delighted. He told reporters that linking up with Paris was the biggest event in his life to date. 'When we signed her, we were a $90 million company. Now we're going to be $200 million or $300 million company. Paris Hilton gave us a lot of opportunities. We love Paris, we really do.' Bet they do.

Industry sources estimate that Paris's fragrances account for nearly 40 per cent of Parlux's total business. A Parlux licensee, Zone 88 Corporation, is planning on launching the Paris Hilton handbag and Paris has also signed a sunglasses licence agreement. According to a senior source at Parlux, Paris is 'a marketer's dream'.

'She's a very important person in American culture, if not the most important,' said Lekach. 'People love to love her and love to hate her. She's very controversial. When we launched the Paris Hilton fragrance I expected it to do about $20 million. [By year's end] we were doing $50 million in wholesale sales, and we're still rolling out. So I expect to be blown away with the handbags.'

Many were surprised by the success. 'The general belief was that the Paris Hilton name would not lend itself to a hugely profitable and sustainable brand,' said Mark Moeller, a financial analyst. 'What's been proven quarter after quarter is that those people were wrong.' Her father Rick was particularly proud of her success. 'It's not all fun and games for Paris,' Rick said. 'But she's done things slowly. She hasn't tried to spread herself too thin with business ventures that don't make sense.'

Hilton says she wears her own perfume all the time and chose the scents from dozens of samples.' If my name is on something, I want it to be something I can wear,' Hilton said. Soon, though, she was adding a men's fragrance to her line. She announced this intention in February 2005 and made a bold promise to potential purchasers. 'It's so hot that when guys wear it, it makes girls want them.'

Paris hoped that another thing that girls would want to get their hands on was her own range of watches. With the help of design companies Parlux and Tourneau she's designed a glamorous time-piece from 1,000 diamonds that shows five time zones – very jet-set! – and carries a hefty price tag of £100,000. 'I worked with the watchmakers and designed the entire watch and the box it came in,' Hilton boasted. 'It has two of my favorite things: diamonds and travel.' Asked about the expensive price, Paris revealed that she had plans to launch a more affordable version. 'I'm going to have watches in all different price ranges, so all my fans and anyone can afford them,' she said.

A firm believer in doing good by doing good, Paris – who earned an estimated £200,000 from the watch endorsement deal – decided to auction the first edition of her watch for charity. Held at the Antiquorum auction house on Madison Avenue, Manhattan in November 2005, the auction attracted a great deal of attention. Oscar Rodriguez, the boss of an online diamond jewellery retailer, Abazias, paid $125,000 for the watch at a live charity auction. Proceeds of the charity auction, hosted by Parlux Fragrance and Tourneau went to the

Memorial Sloan Kettering for Breast Cancer Research. 'We are thrilled to have participated in this event,' says Rodriguez. 'Abazias and Paris Hilton share a special bond. We showcase over 70,000 diamonds and it's very possible that she does too!'

Next up in Paris's commercial life was a book. News that Paris was hawking around a book proposal was first broken the *Daily News* on 22 January 2004. 'You've seen the movie, now read the book: Paris Hilton is shopping a literary proposal that is expected to bring in around $1 million,' screamed the report. Within weeks Paris had signed a deal with Simon & Schuster imprint Fireside. 'Obviously, the public is fascinated by her,' said Trish Todd, executive vice president of Touchstone Fireside. 'Ratings for her TV show are fabulous. She's on the cover of every magazine known to man... She's on every red carpet. For girls today, her life would be their fantasy.'

Paris described her work as 'a funny book. It's a look at my life. I talk about boys, dating tips, fashion. It's a fun, comedy book.' She collaborated with ghost-writer Merle Ginsberg to help her *write Confessions Of An Heiress: A Tongue-in-Chic Peek Behind The Pose.* Entertainment journalist and former *W* magazine writer, Ginsberg had previously profiled Boy George and Johnny Cash – he was a very safe pair of hands for a fantastic book.

A total of 115,000 copies were printed for the first run; the book debuted at number 59 on amazon.com and quickly mooched its way up to number 31. In the week of the launch, she appeared at the Times Square branch of

Virgin Megastore to sign copies. 'It's the only reason I came into the city,' said Dave Rubin, 42, of New Jersey, whose purchase of the $17.92 wristband guaranteed him a copy of the book and a chance to meet Paris 'I can't wait to meet her and tell her how funny she is. I'd like to see her stay around in the public eye for a long time. She's just a fascinating person.'

'Paris is becoming so popular, she only has to go by her first name,' said a 20-year-old female fan as she looked around. 'When people hear the word Paris, they think of her.' The lady of the hour arrived three minutes early and signed copies, adding a cartoon heart next to each signature. When she complimented one woman on the colour of her blouse, the ecstatic fan bounced out of the queue in joy. 'She said she liked it,' screamed Rebekkah Abraham, 20, of Brooklyn, as she pushed her glasses back up her nose. 'She's so fashionable, and yet she liked it!'

The following stop on Paris's promotional tour was an appearance at the Wal-Mart store in Stevenson Ranch, Los Angeles. Blue posters were plastered over the city and a bright pink banner was draped over the entrance to Wal-Mart – the store Paris had so amused everyone with by pretending she didn't know what it was in *The Simple Life*. Those who queued up for the chance to see Paris included 37-year-old Michael Swartzburg of northern California. He had driven 300 miles and stayed at a local hotel overnight to guarantee a good place in the queue. He arrived at Wal-Mart at 5 a.m. dressed in a black-tie outfit.

'It's a special occasion and if you're going to meet

someone who personifies fashion, you had better be somewhat fashionable yourself,' he said shortly before Paris took her place in front of a pink backdrop, strewn with pink and white balloons. She was wearing a white, strapless mini-dress. Swartzburg was with Paris just 20 seconds as she signed his two copies of the book but that was enough to send the 37-year-old on to cloud nine. 'Those 20 seconds were possibly the best relationship I've ever had,' he said. 'Short, but meaningful. She just has a Marilyn Monroe presence about her. This whole thing was well worth it.'

She subsequently turned up at venues across America to promote and sign her book. At one signing in California, she was described by one reporter as 'looking like and explosion in a florist's shop' in her shocking pink outfit. More shocking, though, was her appearance at West Hollywood's Book Soup store, at which two men threw eggs at her. 'Paris was very shaken and could not believe it when the crowd started chanting and hurling abuse,' said an onlooker. 'All of a sudden two blokes threw eggs at her head but they missed and cracked on her shoulder. Paris had to be shielded by eight bodyguards and was really upset.' She had the last laugh, however, when she noticed shortly afterwards that a huge billboard of her had brought traffic to a standstill on Sunset Boulevard. In the leggy photograph she was modelling Guess clothes designed by Marciano. Not one to dwell on things, she later danced her troubles away the Music Box nightclub in Hollywood.

With the promotional tour over, her editor at Fireside, Trish Todd, was pleasantly surprised by the turnout at the signings. 'We thought it was mostly going to be teenage girls,' she said. 'But it was moms with strollers, it was little old ladies, it was gay guys, it was businessmen in suits – it was everyone.' The book spent five weeks on the *New York Times* bestseller list in 2004. The success of it was a nice two-fingered salute to those who had scoffed at the very idea of Paris writing a book. For the intellectually snobbish, Paris represents much of what they dislike, and for this girl to write a book when many of those who have mocked her have not managed to do so must have been particularly painful.

Not only has Paris written a book, she's also read quite a few too, 'Contrary to what people think,' she writes in Confessions. She then lists a number of 'tomes' that she has enjoyed including *The Great Gatsby* by F. Scott Fitzgerald, *The Best of the Best Dressed List* by Jackie Collins, *Sex And The City* and *Four Blondes* by Candace Bushnell, *Maneater* by Gigi Levangie Grazer and Plum Syke's *Bergdorf Blondes*.

Confessions received some positive comments in reviews. The *Tribune* said: 'It's an heiress diary for us regular Joes. Now we can all pretend like we're spoiled-rotten socialites, too.' The *Boston Herald* added: 'The wit and wisdom of Hilton is sprinkled throughout.' The *Chicago Sun Times* suggested: 'Stuck for a gift this year, just think Paris!' Meanwhile, the *Green Bay Press Gazette* chimed: 'Not since the *Diary of Anne Frank* has a journal examined the complications and struggles of everyday life so intimately. It's all here: Paris' plans, dreams, secrets, favourite designers, career goals and tips on meeting cute guys. Laugh all you want, but there's nothing easy about posing for the paparazzi or dating Greek shipping heirs.' The *Contra Costa Times* was more literal: '*Your Heiress Diary: Confess It All To Me* lets her fans (there are some, right?) have their very own heiress diary. Just in time for the holidays, the pink tome is full of pictures of Paris.'

Paris and her mother were special guests at the 35th Los Angeles gay pride event in Hollywood. Arriving in her dark-green custom-built Ferrari, she was dressed in a yellow-gold beaded gown and had Tinkerbell in her hand. Her mother was wearing white trousers, a white hat and white Chanel sunglasses. A drag queen shouted to Paris, 'Hi, sexy! You're gorgeous! I love you!' Paris replied, 'Thanks, bitch!'

She later said of the participants, 'I love the gay community. I love you guys. I love your style.' Indeed, she has always been a fan of gay people who she believes are more fun, better dressers and better lookers than their heterosexual male equivalents. Paris's feelings for the gay community are widely reciprocated in that community. Her glamorous, eventful lifestyle, hedonistic nature and string of gorgeous celebrity boyfriends have had gay men looking up to her for years. The fact that she occasionally gets her claws out when discussing other women doesn't hurt her cause either. She has, after all, called Jessica Simpson 'fat', Hilary Swank 'ugly' and Sharleen Spiteri 'a f*cking ugly idiot'. It's also believed that she sent Nicole Richie a biscuit to taunt her about her weight problems. Meanwhile, she accused her detractor, pop singer Pink, of using her to attempt a comeback when she mocked Paris in the video for her song *Stupid Girls*. 'Like, f*ck her. That's like totally out of order and I just don't get it.'

Gay commentator Mark Simpson says of Paris's appeal, 'Since many young gays still need to identify with 'strong women', or at least successful ones, Paris Hilton seems to offer a template of feminine success and glamour that is much less scary than, say, Madonna. Paris is cool where Madonna is sweaty. Or Britney is bonkers. The name Paris Hilton is also quite gay, no?'

As so many people were enjoying the glimpse that *Confessions* gave into the celebrity lifestyle, Paris was unwittingly the source for a much closer glimpse when a teenager hacked into Paris's mobile phone account and discovered the phone numbers for hundreds of celebrities. He then posted them on the Internet for all to see. This led to several friends of hers being bombarded with phone calls.

A spokesperson for her phone company said: 'T-Mobile is investigating the reported disclosure of Paris Hilton's information. T-Mobile's computer forensics and security team is actively investigating to determine how Ms Hilton's information was obtained. This includes the possibility that someone had access to one of Ms Hilton's devices and/or knew her account password.'

Publicist Tara Solomon, 46, who worked with Paris on

promotional events and whose telephone number is therefore programmed into Hilton's phone, fielded nearly 100 calls. 'All young guys. Different area code every time. The phone rang constantly, every five to 10 minutes.' In the end she had to switch if off just to be able to get to sleep. Other celebs to be inundated with calls included indie film producer Vallen Smikle Jr, who received over 80 calls, and Henry Quintero, 34, an exec assistant with MTV Latin America who works with Casares. He received calls 'from all over the globe. Groups of girls laughing.' One caller, he says, 'congratulated me for being in Paris's phone book.'

'I got 100 calls in two hours,' said reality television star Victoria Gotti. 'I didn't want to take the phones off the hook because my oldest son was out on a date. This went on all night. Finally, at 5:30 a.m., I took them off the hook. This morning, I put them back on and they started ringing immediately. It's driving me insane.'

Ouch! Embarrassing times for Paris. 'I want to apologize to all my friends and family,' she said. Referring implicitly back to the Salomon affair she said that she felt 'horrible that, once again, someone has invaded my privacy.' And once again, the Internet had played a part in humiliating Paris.

In September 2005, a 17-year-old Massachusetts' boy was sentenced to 11 months in a juvenile facility after pleading guilty at the US District Court in Boston to nine counts of juvenile delinquency. The charges had included hacking into Internet and telephone service providers, theft of personal information and posting it on the Web, and making bomb threats to high schools in Florida and Massachusetts, all over a 15-month period. In addition to his jail term and for two years after his release, the teenager was prohibited from possessing or using any computer, cell phone or other equipment capable of accessing the Internet.

The following year, somebody hacked into Lindsay Lohan's Blackberry and, according to Lohan's representative, sent 'disgusting and very mean messages that everyone thought were coming from Lindsay. They weren't. We now have her lawyers looking into it. Some people think Paris may have been involved because the wording of the messages sounds very familiar.'

Elliot Mintz was quick to offer his sympathy to Lohan but also to deny that Paris had anything to do with the hacking. 'I'm saddened this happened to Lindsay. I lived through this with Paris two years ago when her Sidekick was hacked into, and the loss of privacy is unbearable. But as for any suggestion that Paris would have anything to do with this, that is silly, untrue and unfortunate.'

Another incident that caused controversy for Paris was an advertisement she filmed for Carl's Jr. hamburger restaurant. The burger chain was delighted to get her to agree to promote their brand. 'Paris was chosen to star in the ad because she is an intriguing cultural icon and the "It girl" of the moment,' said marketing chief Brad Haley. 'She fascinates Carl's Jr.'s most loyal customers, "young, hungry guys," as well as "young, hungry gals".' He explained that the advertisement featuring Paris was more like a music video than a typical television commercial. 'The message is very simple: Paris, the situation, and the Spicy BBQ Six Dollar Burger are "hot".'

In the controversial advertisement, Paris mooches into a garage wearing just high heels and a sexy black swimsuit and takes a sponge and soaps her scantily clad body. She then suggestively sprays the camera with a hose and writhes over a black Bentley, to the soundtrack of *I Love Paris In The Spring Time*. She brings matters to a climax by biting into one of the burgers and declaring 'That's hot'.

The backlash was quick in coming. 'This commercial is basically soft-core porn,' spat Melissa Caldwell, research director for the Parents Television Council. 'It's inappropriate for television.' Stuart Fischoff, a media psychologist, predicted that the advertisement would hurt the company. 'This could come back and bite them on the behind. We're in the throes of a culture war in this country, and for them to be pushing the envelope like this, at this time, could be very dangerous.'

The *Sun* newspaper was more positive when they covered the story: 'Nice Baps, Paris,' admired their headline. Brad Haley was unrepentant in the face of the controversy. He said on the company's Website that the concept was: 'Great-looking actress, great-looking car, great-looking burger, that's pretty much the idea.' Claudia Caplan, chief marketing officer for the agency that designed the commercial said, 'Look, we're never going to have McDonald's advertising budget or Burger

King's budget. Whatever we do has to have an effect that is multiplied over several platforms. It needs to be more than just a television commercial.' The same agency had faced controversy in the past for an advertisement featuring a woman sitting on a slowly grinding mechanical bull while eating a burger.

The advertisement got the thumbs up from business commentator David Kiley, who wrote on his blog, 'As the father of a corruptible three year old, I should abhor the racy TV ad by Carl's Jr. featuring a scantily clad Paris Hilton sudsing up a Bentley to the tune of *I Love Paris In The Spring Time*, right? Sorry. Despite protests from parent watchdog groups, like The Parents Television Council, this is just plain smart marketing in today's world. Was it tacky? Sure. Paris Hilton is a curious pop culture phenomenon that is hot with young, edgy fast-food eaters. Is the whole thing effective? For me, it works better than Oprah's giveaway of Pontiacs on her show.'

In September 2004, the next arm of the Paris Hilton business chain was launched in the shape of an exclusive jewellery range sold through the Amazon Website. Amazon created a special online Paris Hilton Boutique, where customers were able to see photographs of Hilton wearing the designs. It was a classy move for an online book store.

'I grew up surrounded by the finest fashion and jewellery designs, and I really wanted to create a line that was beautiful and very high quality, yet affordable and available to everyone,' said Paris. 'Amazon.com is the perfect place to launch the line because customers everywhere can shop for it – whether they live in LA or New York or a very small town. This jewellery is for the heiress in everyone.'

'The Paris Hilton Collection is a wonderful addition to the Amazon.com jewellery store,' said Eric Broussard, then Amazon.com's vice president of Jewellery & Watches. 'The boutique on Amazon.com offers a blend of entertainment and shopping that customers can't find elsewhere, including beautiful images of Paris wearing the jewellery that could be from the pages of a fashion magazine, as well as a personal video message from Paris.' All items purchased from the Paris Hilton Collection were delivered to customers in a midnight-blue velvet jewellery pouch, and included a keepsake card with a note from Paris featuring her signature tiara logo.

The collection quickly became a top seller on Amazon, and within months five new items were added – a charm bracelet, pendant, dangle earrings, a belly bar and a pet collar. Paris was delighted with the success of her range. 'Fans have been so thrilled with my Amazon.com jewellery line that I wanted to create even more designs for them to enjoy,' she said, beaming. 'In addition to my own sense of style, I think a lot of people admire Tinkerbell's look, which is why I decided to include a glamorous pet collar as part of the new collection.'

With that collection on the shelves, it was time for Paris to get back to basics and hit the road…

10

THE SHOW
MUST GO ON

In the summer of 2004, *The Simple Life* was back – this time on a hilarious cross-country road trip! The girls drove their pink trailer from Miami to Beverly Hills and were again separated from their mobile phones, cash and credit cards. 'Think Lucy and Ricky in long trailers or Chevy Chase in Vacation,' said executive producer Jon Murray. 'This is a natural for Paris and Nicole,' Murray added. 'They've spent most of their vacations in the South of France, London or Tokyo. They've never done a cross-country vacation.' Further excitement was forthcoming. 'It'll be interesting to see the country through their eyes,' added Mike Darnell, Fox's executive vice president of special programming. 'Maybe Paris will visit a Wal-Mart. I'm kind of hoping they stop at a Hilton.'

In the opening episode, Paris and Nicole were on the final day of a holiday on South Beach, Miami. They are told their limousine has been confiscated and in its place they are presented with a pink pick-up truck and caravan trailer. 'The last time we had the blue truck and we ended up painting it pink so this time they gave us a pink one to start with. Pink is my favourite colour,' said Paris. Leaving behind their luxurious lifestyles, they hit the road for a month-long road trip. 'I drove the whole time,' Hilton said. 'It's really hard, tugging along a 25-foot trailer. It was scary going on the highways.' The first stop is at the Batten family ranch where a terrifying accident befell Paris.

While filming a scene in Florida, Paris was thrown from the horse she was riding. To make matters worse, the horse then kicked her in the stomach and her thigh. 'It feels like spikes going inside,' Paris sobbed after hitting the ground. She was immediately airlifted to hospital and given intravenous therapy, which was really painful. She spent three hours in hospital being examined. She underwent everything including CAT scans, MRI and other tests.

'To err on the absolute side of caution, we made a decision to medevac her to a hospital in Tampa,' said Chris Alexander, a spokesman for 20th Century Fox Television. 'We're hoping she's fine,' he told reporters, adding, 'Whenever you're dealing with talent, you always want to be extra careful.'

The press claimed that she was thrown from the horse because she was wearing high heels. This isn't true; she was actually wearing tennis shoes. 'I've been riding horses my whole life and this has never happened to me, ever,' she told reporters outside the hospital. 'Luckily there was no internal bleeding.' Paris was given two days off filming and spent the time in bed. It had been a terrifying experience for her and she took the time to relax and take a look at where she was in life. However, just as it's said people should 'get back on the horse', she was soon back in front of the camera.

In the second episode, Paris bounced back and worked at the Weeki Wachee Springs mermaid water park in Florida. She performed as a show mermaid while Nicole tried to take the role of a turtle. The pair went on to work as maids at a nudist colony and then rolled up their sleeves at a sausage factory. They are horrified to discover how sausages are made. At this point they are staying with the Skinner family, whose son James has offended Nicole. The pair make a special sausage for James – filled with dog food.

Next up for Paris and Nicole came the swamps of Louisiana where they stayed with Laurette and Mitch Mequet at Cypress Cove Landing, the Mequet's houseboat rental business on the Atchafalaya Basin. The couple are able to give a good insight into how Paris and Nicole behaved on and off camera. On arrival, Laurette encouraged them to smell the region's fresh air. 'It smells like shit,' barked Nicole. 'The director said "Cut",' remembers Laurette. 'They could tell from my face, when I turned, I wasn't happy. If [Nicole] had been closer, I could have just thrown her in. She apologized and said, 'It really does smell good.' But we had to do that part again.'

'They perform for the camera,' said Mitch Mequet. 'When it's showtime, they know what they have to do. It's a comedy, reality show, so they get paid to be comical. But they're not what they portray. One example – they came from Mississippi with red bug bites. They were scared to ask for medication because they were itching. Laurette offered to rub the bites with some medication. They were amazed we would do that for them, but they were treated like they were our kids.'

There was wider amazement at the couple for agreeing to get involved in the show in the first place. 'We've had some people say, "I can't believe y'all let these people come here and make fun of us",' said Mitch. 'We don't want to be made fun of, but people have to understand this is a comedy reality show.

'For me and Laurette, it's our nature to have fun and be comical at times. We have a good time. But I don't think their goal was to come out and make fun of our culture. I think they wanted to be part of our culture.' The Mequets enjoyed the experience and said Nicole and Paris even asked to come back, off camera, to experience more swamp life. The Mequets would like that, too. 'I'd like for them to get a feel for what we do as a family,' said Laurette. 'I'd want them to get the true meaning of the area. If they could have stayed longer, we would have had them slide down the levee on some cardboard, take them swimming on the river. That's stuff we did with our kids and they remember them.'

Other highlights in the series included the time that Paris and Nicole went to a nudist resort in Florida. They worked as maids there and Paris found herself in the strange position of being the least exhibitionist person in a community! She admits she found being around so many nude people very strange, particularly when they wanted to have their photographs taken with her and Nicole. 'Ewww,' Paris said. 'I've never seen old people naked before. It was gross.' She told David Letterman, 'Everyone is nude all the time – when they're eating, when they're bike riding, you name it. It's disgusting.'

In an earlier interview, she said, 'It was really gross. It wasn't like a nudist colony with people our age or anyone, like, really hot.' Nicole agreed. "I have no problem with nudity at all. But all the people there were all really old. Sometimes we would see people riding their bikes. They had tops on but no bottoms. I can understand going topless, but bottomless? It's perverted.' Some members of the nudist colony, on hearing of Paris's words, reminded her that one day she and Nicole, too, would be old.

Paris was also less than delighted to be working in a sausage factory. 'I never knew sausage was made out of strings of slimy pig intestines,' she confessed in *Confessions*. 'They look like condoms and you have to push the meat through to make sausage. I swear I'll never eat sausages again. Even at the Ivy. Okay, maybe at the Ivy.' Paris says the worst part of the second series was that they had to beg for money. She deliberately got Nicole to do most of the work with the begging while she just stood back and looked pretty. 'I know what I'm good at,' she says.

They also worked as hotel maids for two days. You can imagine how much Paris enjoyed this. In the end, their efforts were somewhat limited and they ended up lying on the hotel bed, ordering room service and gabbing away on the phone. They ape the theme in the film *Maid In Manhattan*, taking off their maids' uniforms and posing as guests. The real maids come in and clean the room while Paris and Nicole lie back in splendour.

Paris was delighted by all the travelling involved in making the series – which is just as well as there was plenty of it. One day she drove 12 hours straight as the girls headed to Biloxi, Mississippi. There were three cameras in the car at all times and Paris says she genuinely did do the driving. 'I loved Louisiana. We stayed with a family on a swamp. It was, like, all muddy, but the people were so nice. I like Mississippi too. They had a casino, and we went there. I also loved Texas. We just met so many neat people along the way. It was a totally cool experience.'

It was a hectic schedule for her and she was not allowed to keep in such close contact with her family and friends as she would normally be able to do. 'We had one day off on Sundays so you'd make your calls then. Basically, we'd go to the mall, to a movie. That was nice. But I'm used to having my cell phone glued to my ear.'

Neither was the programme-making progress

particularly tranquil. At a trailer park in Ocean Springs, Mississippi, the girls reportedly had an argument that went on for hours. One crew member claimed, 'They got so bored they ended up ripping into each other. In the end Paris screamed, "That's it! I'm never working with that **** again!" She and Nicole regularly got drunk and ended up in a screaming match.'

With the argument over, more of the thinking behind the show was revealed by the programme-makers. The choice of Florida and Texas for the filming locations had been taken for the simple reason of the girls' wardrobes. 'Quite honestly, we went there for the weather,' executive producer Jonathan Murray admits. 'We knew it was going to give Paris and Nicole the opportunity to dress the way they usually like to dress, which is usually with very few clothes.'

Murray also commented on the development of the format, from the first season. 'Last season, we came up with this idea of the crazy sound effects we use. We sort of punctuate, tell the audience, 'Oh, this is funny' or 'This is a weird moment.' This season, we had an extra camera – always one on the persons Paris and Nicole were dealing with and one on them. So we were able to get reaction shots that helped with the comedy, which made editing easier.'

Murray was also asked once again the golden question that hung over every season of *The Simple Life*: to what extent were Paris and Nicole pretending to act dumb rather than actually being dumb. 'The times when they might try to be funny, those are things that may or may not work. We find the best stuff just happens because they're Paris and Nicole. Sometimes it's sort of fun because you're not sure. When Paris puts the metal pot in the microwave, you're going, "Does she really not know you don't do that?"'

However, Murray admits that there were often times when the girls were less than delighted to be taking part in the show. 'Well, they certainly love doing the publicity,' he said. 'They certainly love walking the red carpet. They love all of that. But being on a road trip for 30 days, the novelty for them wore off pretty quickly.

'They did not enjoy going to bed in that trailer each night. And that's part of what made the show good. And we just had to keep saying, "No, you need to do that." But it's amazing as I look at the tape, there are a lot of times when they're having a great time together, although they both would say, "Oh, I'd never want to do that again."'

Paris says she learned a great deal from the second season. 'I have never really had a job so I had no idea. It's a lot of work. I do acting and modelling. Those are work but this is very different. It makes you respect everyone around you, and think about how you treat people. There are some people who are rude to waiters and waitresses. Like some of my friends in LA. I see how they are, how they feel some people are beneath them just because they're working to make a living. I have never done that. I try to be nice to everyone… It's very hard and we should give them respect for doing it. I could not imagine waking up every day and doing any of those jobs.'

Just as she found the work mentally and physically taxing, she also found the driving physically draining. 'It was so difficult to drive the trailer,' Paris says. 'It was really hard. Especially making big turns or backing up, I always wanted someone to help me… but we couldn't let the crew help us, so I'd have to ask some random person. On the freeway, when it was windy, the trailer would rock back and forth. Nicole and I shared the same bed, and clothes were thrown everywhere. It was just a total mess, because it was so small.'

Fresh from being voted 'One Of The 10 Most Fascinating People of 2004' by ABC's Barbara Walters, Paris appeared again on the small screen in the third series of *The Simple Life*. Though not before controversy had surrounded the plans for the series. The programme-makers had hoped to film one episode at Cleary Middle School, performing tasks such as substitute teaching and cafeteria duty. However, parents erupted and protested against the plans. 'We initially thought it was a hoax,' said Buena Regional School District Superintendent Diane DeGiacomo. 'They told us that an administrator could stand outside the door with earphones on and, as soon as they heard something that was not appropriate, they could walk in.'

However, after the protests, the idea was scrapped. 'I'm happy to hear that this isn't going to happen and this isn't going to tarnish our community in any way. It just wasn't appropriate for this setting,' said Buena Vista Mayor Chuck Chiarello.

The girls travelled around the northeast United States by Greyhound Bus. They tried their hands at being everything from mechanics to mortuary workers, zoo-keepers, nursing home attendants and dentists, all under the banner of 'Interns'. In one episode, mother-of-three Joyce Brower welcomed the girls into her home in New Jersey. On learning how heartbroken Brower had been over the death of her dog, they bought two huge Great Danes from a breeder, named them Flea and Billy and took them to the Brower household. At the end of the show, the breeder turned up at Joyce's door demanding £1,000 for each animal. In the end, Joyce gave them back.

Animal chaos is to the fore in another episode, when the girls stayed with a family who own several species of monkey. An orangutan leapt on to the bed Paris was sitting on and sneaked a look up her skirt. 'I've had plenty of men trying to look up my skirt but never a monkey,' said Paris, laughing the incident off. 'I couldn't keep the thing away from me – but he was cute and I grew attached to him in the end.'

Turning their attentions to the airline industry, they prove to be hilariously disastrous baggage handlers. They worked for the now-defunct Southeast Airlines. Airport officials agreed to allow Hilton and Richie to film in Hanover Township, Lehigh County, because they though it would be good publicity. Paris and Nicole throw luggage on to the runway and open up suitcases to try on the passengers' clothes. They then become air-hostesses, a task they are predictably much better equipped to pull off. 'We love you bitches,' they say over the cabin intercom. They feel a bit icky, though, when they have to clean the airliner's toilets with an enormous vacuum cleaner. 'It's like a colonic,' says Nicole.

Perhaps the most controversial episode came when Paris and Nicole worked at a mortuary. They drove a hearse, filled in a grave and held a mock funeral. In the most contentious scene, they spilled what appeared to be human ashes on to a carpet, then used a vacuum cleaner to clean them up. Local residents were outraged. 'It was totally tacky,' said Amy Van Dalinda, who said the mock funeral was in the same room where her late father had been laid out, 'which was really horrible for me.' The 'human ashes' were actually a mixture of cat litter and cement, according to John Podesta, the owner of the mortuary. A disclaimer at the end of the show said no human bodies were used in any of the scenes.

In other episodes they work at a television station and read the weather live on air, change nappies at a daycare centre, make an enormous mess at a bakery, plan weddings and work as psychics. They also work at a dentist's office where they slap numbed-up patients, put make-up on them, and make prank calls. Their journey ends with a welcome home party in New York as they return to their less-than-simple lives. It was a fantastic series and marked one of the final times that Paris and Nicole would be portrayed together on good terms, before their friendship came to an end.

11

MAD ABOUT THE BACKSTREET BOY

Nick Carter is a world-famous celebrity thanks to his membership of the Backstreet Boys who have sold over 80 million albums. With his floppy blonde hair and boyish features, he is a pin-up for girls around the globe. In 1999, he was ranked No. 1 on the list of 'Hottest Under 21' by *Teen Scene* magazine and was named 'The Biggest Teen Idol' by *Teen People* magazine. He was voted one of *People* magazine's '50 Most Beautiful People' in 2000, then in 2002, the readers of *Cosmo* magazine voted him 'The Sexiest Man in the World'.

Carter was born the year before Paris but like her, he seemed destined for stardom from an early age. He took small parts in movies and then joined the Backstreet Boys at the age of just 12. Another thing they had in common were ambitious siblings: Nick's younger brother Aaron has become a famous pop singer, heart-throb and actor.

Finally, like Paris, Carter has starred in a reality television show – *House Of Carters*, though this started filming after the couple split up.

'I tend to fall for guys who are cool,' writes Paris in *Confessions*. 'One thing that always attracts me: guys who can sing. I think a guy who can sing is really sexy. Singing is the hardest thing to do because it's so easy to get embarrassed – singing takes confidence. I admit I'm also attracted to pretty-boy male models.' Well in Carter she had found a boyfriend who could sing and who had the sort of pretty-boy looks that could have taken him far in the modelling world.

The relationship between Paris and Nick first hit the headlines in December 2003. 'A backstreet beau for Paris' ran the story in the *New York Post*. Within days she was spotted smooching with Carter in a Beverly Hills alleyway. As the press continued to track the golden couple's movements, Carter owned up. 'We've been kind of seeing each other for three weeks now,' he said. 'It was right after Christmas that I started hanging out with her... I met her, and it kind of kicked it off. I really like her. She is cool to hang out with, she's got a really good personality, and she's outgoing. You know, it's funny because our personalities are really similar. It works. You know, at the end of the day, I'm having fun with her; I enjoy spending time with her. She's a sweetheart.'

Sounds idyllic, doesn't it? However, after the pair split, his account of the early days of their relationship became more graphic. 'She made it clear she wanted to have sex and couldn't keep her hands off me,' he said. 'At the start she loved to tease me by saying she wasn't wearing any pants. But because I know Paris is used to getting what she wants when she wants, I was determined to make her wait, which drove her wild with desire. In fact I held out for three weeks before I had sex with her.'

The pair were spotted together at the Sundance Film Festival. They seemed to be having a ball, dancing on tables at a nightclub before Paris took to the stage and sang *Hello*, by Lionel Richie. All seemed to be going well. A source close to Paris told the British press, 'Paris and Nick get on so well; they're totally loved up. When they are together they can't keep their hands off each other. Paris really wants to be taken seriously and Nick does that. Since they've been together he has really helped calm down her wild partying and has a tremendous effect on her.'

Paris first met Carter through her bodyguard, who is a friend of Carter's. The bodyguard let him know that Paris was interested in him. Carter was naturally very interested but first asked the advice of his fellow band member AJ McLean. 'Paris Hilton keeps calling me,' McLean remembers Carter saying one night at West Hollywood hotspot Chi. McLean replied, 'Just have fun and enjoy it.' It seems they did indeed have fun and soon Paris was hinting that they might marry. She told a reporter, 'I want to get married in the next couple of years. Definitely.'

At the beginning of July, they had tattoos to cement

their relationship. Carter got 'Paris' on his wrist but would not confirm what Paris chose. However these tattoos could not cover the problems that were developing between them. They were seen arguing at a party given by Jay-Z at the PlayStation 2 Estate on 4 July to launch his new trainer line. They had a row by the pool and Paris shouted at Carter, 'Come on, put down that drink!' They also had a row during a night out in Hollywood. An onlooker said, 'She was crying in the corner and people were trying not to look. She cut a very lonely figure. But then her ex-fiancé Jason Shaw put his arm around her and her bodyguard suggested she should leave. And grudgingly, she put one foot in front of another.'

It came as little surprise, then, when it was announced soon after this that Paris had split from Carter. A spokesperson confirmed the split, adding, 'She's concentrating on her work.' Carter was the first of the two to speak publicly about the split. 'No, I don't regret it because I love her. She'll have a place in my heart, always.' He told *People* magazine, 'Our relationship totally was based on distrust. She didn't trust me. I didn't trust her.' The interviewer asked straight out if he thought Paris had cheated on him. 'The only comment I'm going to have to that is that I'm loyal to those who are loyal to me,' replied Carter.

Paris set the record straight when she said, 'I'm a faithful girlfriend. I never cheat. It's so wrong to do that when you're intimate with another person. The papers would say, 'Paris was with this actor, and they were kissing.' At first, he was upset, but at the end of the day, Nick knew the rumours weren't true.' Her friends were quick to rally round and support her. 'I certainly didn't like him,' said Casey Johnson, heiress to the Johnson & Johnson fortune and friend of Paris. 'I think that having Nick was bringing her down,' she said. 'She didn't have time for both. He needed a lot of attention.'

Clearly the relationship had not always been smooth sailing. 'When they were really good, they were great, and when they were bad, they were awful,' said a friend of Paris. Even more alarmingly, a week after the split, Paris was photographed at Los Angeles International Airport with a bruised arm and a split lip. Speculation immediately began that she had sustained the injuries from the hand of Carter.

The day after the photographs were published, she attended a charity polo match at Bridgehampton but kept a low profile, sitting inside a vehicle with tinted windows and wearing oversized sunglasses. When asked by a reporter how Paris was feeling, Hilton family spokeswoman Catherine Saxton said, 'She's fine, she's absolutely fine.' When asked about the speculation about Paris's injuries, Saxton said, 'There will be no comment.'

The Backstreet Boy, however, strenuously denies that he ever assaulted Paris. He said, 'I'll tell you one thing: I didn't touch her. I'm not that kind of guy. I would never do that.' His former girlfriend Angi Taylor came out in his defence, saying, 'The Nick I knew would never lay a hand on a woman, especially a woman he loves.' Paris has never claimed that Carter hit her nor has she ever taken legal action against him because of her injuries. When her friend, pro-skateboarder and DJ Chad Muska, asked her how she came by the injuries, she told him, 'I bumped into something'.

Later, Carter would turn sour on Paris in interviews he gave. 'I thought the fact she had money and was famous meant I wouldn't have to worry about somebody using me. Wrong. I kind of fell head over heels for this girl. And I probably shouldn't have. And I would never lay a hand on a woman.' He also admitted cheating on Paris with Ashlee Simpson. 'I hooked up with Ashlee. When Paris came back from Australia, they talked to each other and she found out.' Carter had told Simpson that he and Paris had already split up. As he sought to promote his *House Of Carters* television series, Carter's accusations became more incredible. 'In the very beginning, you know, she was literally cleaning my carpet in my apartment … trying to act all domesticated. And then, before you know it, a month or two goes by and it's back to the old nose up in the air and who are you?'

Nasty stuff from Carter, who covered up his Paris tattoo with a new one showing a skull and crossbones. In his time, Carter also has dated The O.C. starlet Willa Ford as well as actress Bai Ling. He claims that both times, the relationships ended because the women were 'possessive' and 'jealous'. In its guide to finding a good boyfriend, the *Chicago Sun Times* placed a series of famous men in either the 'boyfriend' or 'boyfiend' category. Carter, who has accused Paris of 'trying to destroy him', was placed firmly in the latter.

As for Paris herself, well she is not one to dwell on the past. Before long, she had bounced back and was partying like only she knows how. She let her hair down at a series of family events at the Hamptons at the end of July. As she danced on the banquettes at the Jet East venue, it showed the world that despite her break-up with Carter, she was only looking forward. In nearly every media interview she grants, she is asked about her relationship with Carter. She nearly always refuses to go over old ground.

Her friend Chad Muska comforted her after the split and according to some reports, the pair dated for a while. She was spotted dancing with him at Joseph's nightclub in LA and then a few weeks later, wearing short turquoise skirt and stockings, she arrived with him at Hollywood nightclub Prey. However, that night she left not with Muska but with Limp Bizkit frontman Fred Durst. As for Carter, he still seems to be stuck in the past. One of his most recent pronouncements on Paris was given to the *News Of The World*. 'The only thing that made her happy was her own reflection,' he said. 'She spends so much time looking at herself in the mirror telling herself how gorgeous she is.' But she is, Nick!

It wasn't long before another musician set his sights on Paris, when it was announced she would co-present the MTV Awards in Miami with rocker Lenny Kravitz. 'Lenny thinks she's so sexy and he's arranging to hook up with her for dinner,' said a friend of Kravitz in the run-up to the big night. Paris wore a peachy see-through dress at the awards show, which passed off without any of the controversies that had plagued previous shows. At one point, Paris said to her co-presenter, 'I'm going to try to talk now', and that was about as exciting as it got.

The next man in Paris's life was a tennis player. While out shopping in West Hollywood with Nicky, she told reporters, 'I've got a new man and I'm head over heels in love. I adore him. He's so hot. His name is Mark Philippoussis.' Born in Australia in November 1976, Philippoussis – who regards himself as both Greek and Australian – turned professional in 1994. Standing at 6ft 5in with a powerful physique, his nickname is Scud, because his service and his returns are delivered so hard.

It was said to be Holly Valance who introduced him to Paris while the two women were filming *National Lampoon: Pledge This!* 'Holly hooked them up and they had a wild night out. Now Mark is Paris's latest obsession,' said a source. However, Philippoussis dodged questions about their relationship. 'I don't talk about my private life.' Given a clear chance to deny reports that he was dating Paris, he snapped, 'I'm not going to say anything. I have nothing to say now.' Why would Philippoussis be so coy? Perhaps because he was also dating Delta Goodrem, the Australian singer-songwriter? Goodrem had recently beaten cancer with the help of the tennis player and had released a song, *Out Of The Blue* about the support he gave her. No surprise, then, that he was a little sensitive about reports linking him to Paris.

Goodrem accepted that her long-distance relationship with Philippoussis made things hard for them. Paris was quick to write off the couple's relationship, however. 'That is completely over,' she said. 'Mark says after a while it became obvious Delta was too boring.' Fortunately, Goodrem did not hear the news via Paris's less-than-diplomatic statement. Instead, she heard it in a phone-call from her mother. Not that the method of delivery made the message any less of a blow. A spokesperson for Goodrem said, 'Delta was devastated. As far as she is concerned she and Mark are still an item. She tried to get hold of him, but couldn't.'

Soon after this, it was a case of 'new balls please' for Paris when she was spotted snogging another tennis player, Andy Roddick, in the Light nightclub in Las Vegas. American tennis star Roddick is a former world number one. He is also something of a celebrity having guest-starred on *Sabrina, The Teenage Witch* and hosted an edition of *Saturday Night Live*. He also has a signature fragrance under his name with Parlux. No wonder he and Paris got it together – they had plenty in common.

With the newspapers full of reports of Paris's latest romantic foray into the sporting world, another leading athlete expressed a preference for her. Ronaldinho is widely considered to be the greatest footballer in the world and has recently surpassed David Beckham as the most marketable. Reports suggested that Paris is a firm favourite of the Brazilian football ace and that he was keen to get her to come and enjoy his ball skills. As Posh and Becks disappear towards the sunset, a love match between Paris and Ronaldinho could be huge. Watch this space.

Meanwhile, Paris had her screen career to think of. In 2005, Paris's mother Kathy followed her into the world of reality television when she appeared in the weekly NBC reality television series *I Want To Be A Hilton*. Described as *The Apprentice* meets *Pygmalion*, the show featured contestants challenging for the chance to live like a Hilton for a year. The winner received a prize package that included a $200,000 trust fund, a new apartment and wardrobe, and the opportunity to live the life of high society for one year.

At first the Hiltons were uncomfortable with the title of the show, which they felt was a little inelegant. However, NBC insisted that the inclusion of the Hilton family name was essential for the success of the show. Paris had a cameo role but was reportedly unimpressed by her mother's foray into television. Whether this was true or not, Paris was able to leave her mother on the small screen because she was headed back to the big screen.

12

THE WAX WORKS

Paris's biggest film role to date was to come in a remake of a classic horror film. As Paris revealed, far from jumping at the next opportunity that came her way she had spent a lot of time waiting for the right film for her. 'I got over 100 scripts and turned down every one until *House Of Wax*,' she revealed. 'It's a summer movie with teenagers going into the woods and having a crazy psychopath kill them.' The one she'd been waiting for, clearly!

The film was a remake of the 1953 classic horror film *House Of Wax*, which was the first 3D film of the 1950s when cinema temporarily went 3D crazy. The original was directed by Andre De Toth and starred Vincent Price; it was itself a remake of a 1933 film called *Mystery Of The Wax Museum*. It was about a mad professor who used wax-covered human bodies in his wax museum and made 57th place on Bravo's 100 Scariest Movie Moments.

Getting such a high-profile name as Paris was of course a huge coup for the filmmakers of the new *House Of Wax*. As one newspaper put it, 'Without Paris Hilton, you'd pretty much slam and bolt the door on *House Of Wax*.' Producer Joel Silver admitted that Paris's profile helped her land the part but denied that it was the most important factor. 'Of course I don't think it will hurt us promotionally,' Silver said, 'but if the casting director wasn't happy with her, she would not have been in the movie. I didn't want to ruin the movie. Fortunately, she's great in it.'

'She impressed everybody – she really did,' agreed co-star Chad Michael Murray. 'She showed up, and she wanted to do her job, and she never complained, and she was nice to everybody… In my opinion, I don't think she embarrasses the film one bit.'

Doing her job entailed playing the part of Paige Edwards who is one of a group of friends who have hit the road to attend a championship college football game. On route they camp out for the night, and take the unwise move of offending a mysterious local redneck. The next morning they discover that their car won't start. Eventually, two of the group end up at a mysterious tourist attraction called the House Of Wax. They discover that the House Of Wax is not what it seems and they must escape before they become the main exhibits. Bloodshed galore ensues.

'They needed the sexy character,' said Paris of her part. 'There's a sexy character in every movie. So I played the

With her famous pet Chihuahua dog, Tinkerbell Hilton.

Inset: In August 2004 Tinkerbell vanished without trace and missing posters were put up, with a reward of $5,000. Happily, Paris and her companion were later reunited.

The third season of *The Simple Life*, subtitled *Interns*, would see Paris and Nicole take various internships with companies along the East Coast of the United States. The girls travelled via the Greyhound Bus company's publicly available bus routes *(above)*.

Below left: Mucking about at a circuit board factory.

Below right: Wearing mechanic's overalls whilst working at a garage.

Above left: Looking happy with her then fiancé and Greek shipping heir Paris Latsis at the Serpentine Summer Party, London, June 2005.

Above right and below: On holiday in Athens, Greece, July 2005.

Expanding the Paris Hilton empire.

Above: The Paris Hilton perfume launch with Ilia Kerach, CEO of Parlux Fragrance Inc. in Los Angeles, December 2004.

Below left: In the studio recording her debut album *Paris,* Florida, August 2005.

Below right: Promoting her album in Tokyo, Japan , August 2006. It sold a respectable 607,375 copies worldwide.

Pictured here with on-off boyfriend Stavros Niarchos III on New Year's Eve in Las Vegas, 2005.

Inset: Close-up of Paris wearing a locket with pictures of them together.

Adding acting onto her CV, Paris has appeared in a number of films.

Above left: Appearing in *House of Wax* with fellow cast members *(left to right)* Robert Richard, Chad Michael Murray, Elisha Cuthbert, Jon Abrahams, Brian Van Holt and Jared Padalecki.

Above right: A still from the film.

Below left: Filming on the set of *Bottoms Up*, April 2005

Below right: With Joel Moore on the set of her new film *The Hottie and the Nottie*, Santa Monica Beach, January 2007.

Above: Paris and Britney Spears shopping in Malibu, California, November 2006.

Britney was full of praise for how much Paris had helped her in the aftermath of her split from Kevin Federline.

Below left: Filming the new series of *The Simple Life* at Paris' home in California, March 2007.

Below right: Getting close with *Desperate Housewives* star Josh Henderson, April 2007.

Above: Paris arriving at the Superior Court, Los Angeles, 4 May 2007. She was sentenced to up to 45 days in jail for violating the terms of her probation.

Inset: The Century Regional Detention Facility in Lynwood, California, the jail chosen by the judge for Paris to serve her 23-day sentence.

Below left: Her police mug shot.

Below right: Displaying her pleasure at her release from jail, 26 June 2007, in front of the world's media.

sexy girl who has a little strip scene, and whatever, every movie needs it. I'm glad to do it.' However, this fails to do justice to her part, which includes a graphic death scene that she pulls off brilliantly, and enjoyed doing so. 'That scene was awesome,' she smiles. 'It was really hard to shoot a spike going through my head. It took two days, and I was filming on night shoots, which are the worst hours ever. But it helped with the character because I was supposed to be cold and miserable and crying. So I was, like, literally crying. I was so miserable. I was like, "Oh, please, just kill me already."'

There were tears off set too, when disaster struck during the making of the film. A huge wax candle fell on to gas burners and gutted the studio. The £4 million blaze also destroyed cameras at the Movie World film complex on Queensland's Gold Coast in Australia. However, Paris had already finished shooting her part and was on her way home when this happened.

Before filming ended, the pressure of the role at one point got to Paris and she admits she had a panic attack one day. She took refuge and solace in the arms of co-star Elisha Cuthbert. 'It was four in the morning,' Cuthbert recalled. 'It's raining, it's miserable outside, and we've got this huge sequence to shoot, and she's not doing good. It's a lot of pressure for someone, especially their first time, and for her it was scary. As an actor, you want all the other actors to give the best performance they can, too. What can I do to help? So I said, "Let's forget everything else, forget it's four in the morning, forget that they're waiting, 'cause they can wait. We're good. Let's sit down, read the lines. Let's go over it, and once we feel comfortable, let's go do it for them." And that's what we did.'

Having been comforted and pep-talked to by Cuthbert, Paris was ready for her scene, which she pulled off well. 'My feet were all cut up,' she remembers. 'It was a real forest, and we were really running through it. I was bumping into trees, and I couldn't see. It was scary. It was pretty brutal, but… it was worth all the running around in the forest and getting killed.'

Not that her part was solely concerned with death. She also had to pull off a sex scene with Robert Ri'chard. 'They're actually playing my single "Screwed" while I was shooting it, and I was like, "I want, I want a close-up," and I only had John, the director there, who I trust,' Paris said. 'And he was just filming, and no one else was there because I was embarrassed, you know, to be dancing and taking my clothes off. I felt so cheesy. But I was doing it to my song, so I felt really sexy, and then I just did it, and it turned out really good.'

Although the film did receive some hostile reviews, several critics agreed with Paris that it turned out really good. The *Times Union* said: 'The early reviewers have been harsh with Miss Hilton… she does exactly what she is required to do in a movie like this, with all the skill, admittedly finite, that is required.' *San Francisco Weekly* gave grudging praise when it said: 'Perhaps the biggest surprise here is that Hilton isn't atrocious.'

THE WAX WORKS

The *York Dispatch* was more fulsome in its applause for Paris. 'She's got the looks for it, with her blinding blondeness and her blatant sex appeal. She runs really well while being chased through the woods at night in a lacy red bra and panties [and does the obligatory face-plant before getting up and scampering away, barefoot]. And she's capable of unleashing a blood-curdling scream en route to her eventual, graphic demise. Like her or not, Paris does generate an undeniable curiosity... When she's on screen, she's the one you watch. When she's off screen, you wonder when she'll come back, and what sorts of vapid things she'll say when she does.'

The *Washington Post* called the film 'Poisoned genius' and the *Times-Picayune* purred that, 'Impressive visual effects help create a truly gripping finale.' The St Paul Pioneer Press insisted that, 'The actors make the characters compelling because, unlike the dolts in many slasher movies, they are resourceful people – right up until the moment they become resourceful candles.'

In England, Johnny Vaughan was not overly impressed but said in the *Sun*, 'For gore aficionados... the murders are worth the wait.' By the time the film came out on DVD several months later, the same newspaper said the film was: 'Surprisingly watchable ... guaranteed to make you jump out of your skin.' The *Daily Star* was more impressed: 'If you fancy being made to jump in terror as the daft but effective story unfolds, sit back and savour the chills and thrills of this hit shocker.' The *Sunday Telegraph* enthused: 'When *House Of Wax* gets going, it races along, with some ... real ghoulish creativity. The final scenes, set in the museum as it melts, are genuinely spectacular.'

Not that Paris only won praise from the critics. She also won three awards for her part: Best Movie Scream Scene and Movie Breakout Performance from *Teen Choice* magazine, and Best Frightened Performance (yes, that's right) from MTV Movie Awards. The film took a relatively modest $12 million on its opening weekend but went on to take $68,766,121 worldwide. This was Paris's biggest movie role to date and she was determined to keep climbing the cinematic ladder.

Fresh evidence of how far Paris's fame had spread came when Paris-wannabes hit the public eye. Had any viewers tuned into the launch show for 2006's *Celebrity Big Brother* on Channel 4 been watching with the sound turned down, they could have been forgiven for thinking that Paris Hilton was among the year's housemates. However, the pretty blonde girl who walked into the house was not Paris but Chantelle Houghton, the first non-celebrity to take part in the series. Her striking resemblance to Paris quickly caught the attention of the press. 'Professional Paris Hilton Lookalike' screamed the *Evening Standard*. 'Chantelle's just like Paris Hilton... only cheaper' added the *Sun*. The *Daily Mail* was even less pleasant: 'Paris Hilton? More like a Travelodge!'

Phil Green, managing director of her glamour model agency Supermodel Ltd confirmed that she had exploited her similarity to Paris. 'What Chantelle does for us is a cross between glamour work and promotions. In the early days she did work for lads' mags,' he said. 'She was thrilled when she got her Page Three. She also did some TV adverts, but has since concentrated more on her work as a Paris Hilton lookalike. She's a lovely, down-to-earth girl – I think she will do really well in the house.' She earned £300 for four hour's work as a Paris lookalike. She would have a Tinkerbell lookalike in the photographs taken by Alison Jackson, a specialist in look-alikes.

She then moved on to Fake Faces. 'Chantelle is perfect as Paris,' said Jez Lee, managing director of the new agency. 'She creates masses of attention whenever she is out shopping. She is a wonderful girl.' However, it seems things did not go quite so smoothly as hoped. 'I only managed to get one booking for her in seven months.' He was as surprised as anyone when he saw her on the Channel 4 reality show. 'I was sat watching the opening of *Celebrity Big Brother*. This girl came out of a limo and I said to my wife, 'I'm sure that's Chantelle Houghton. She was on our books as a Paris Hilton lookalike.

'And, of course, it was her. And as soon as I saw the media were on to her, I phoned up each of my other Paris Hiltons and said, "Do you mind being a Chantelle lookalike?" They said, "Fine." And I'm sure a lot of people now want to be a lookalike to become famous like Chantelle. I've had emails saying, "I don't know who I look like, but…" How can you be a lookalike if you don't look like anyone?'

As the whole lookalike phenomenon spread, people were searching for a lookalike for Chantelle. Jacqueline Blair, a 19-year-old call-centre worker from West Lothian fitted the bill. One of the tabloid papers ran a series of photographs featuring Chantelle the Paris Hilton lookalike, then a lookalike for Chantelle, then a lookalike for that lookalike and so on. Just how far could Paris's fame spread? And just how much like Paris was Chantelle in character? She certainly had a bubbly personality, an ambitious streak and an ability to poke fun at herself. On *Celebrity Big Brother*, she also revealed her favourite things to be 'fake tan, Lionel Richie, rosé wine and popcorn'. Well, the fake tan and Lionel Richie parts are very Paris.

On the show she fell in love with Samuel Preston, the singer from the band The Ordinary Boys. Word had reached Paris about this British look-a-like and she was excited enough by it to suggest a present for Chantelle and Preston when she learned of their engagement. Paris proposed a weekend for the couple with her in – where else – Paris. 'She will arrange the trip when her work commitments die down,' said a spokesperson. 'They will eat in all the best restaurants and see all the romantic sights before taking in a night at the Opera Bastille.'

In America, there was another famous Paris lookalike in the shape of Canadian model Natalie Reid. When she moved to New York and began modelling, Reid was told by a series of photographers that she closely resembled Paris. She started cashing in on her resemblance by getting into exclusive parties, pretending to be Paris. She joined other celebrity impersonators at events like Boston's Ultra fashion show: Dress the Part – How to Get the Hollywood Look for Less. Perhaps in the hope of following in the cinematic footsteps of the real Paris, Reid has also started taking acting lessons in both New York and Los Angeles, and is pursuing a career as a professional actress.

She says that she first encountered the real Paris in a nightclub. 'I saw her and she was shocked by how much we looked alike! Her new boyfriend, the other Greek heir, [Stavros Niarchos] was there and he kept staring at me like he didn't believe it and laughing a little.' Reid also claims that Paris 'invited me to her house in West Hollywood, and we hung out. She was totally in shock, like staring at me and taking a lot of pictures.'

Reid later advertised a beer on huge billboards, because the company couldn't afford the real Paris. She was whisked to the front row of a fashion show by staff that thought she was the real deal. She gets upgraded at airports and told 'the management will take care of the bill' at posh restaurants. She earns between $2,000 and $5,000 per appearance as Paris. However, people are beginning to get wise to it. In February 2007 she was ejected from a fashion show moments before it began after staff cottoned on that it was not the real Paris Hilton.

A friend of Paris told reporters that she was less than impressed by a lot of this lookalike stuff. 'It's a form of stalking. The family has to spend money on lawyers to keep these fakes in their place.' In September 2006, the situation worsened when Reid posed for *Playboy* magazine. Because *Playboy* had failed to convince Paris to strip for their photographer, they simply asked her look-a-like to do so instead. 'Natalie Reid is turning heads throughout the world today as her *Playboy* issue hits the stands,' said a spokesperson for the model. 'We've been bombarded with fan mail and press requests from around the world. Natalie is by far one of the busiest Paris look-a-likes working today and she has become the most famous one of them all, by posing for *Playboy* in the September issue, which hits stands today. If you are looking for Paris Hilton for your next event, try Natalie Reid, the next best Paris.'

However, if it was the real Paris you were after, you could get plenty of her on the Internet video-sharing Website YouTube. In August 2006, she became one of the first celebrities to launch her own channel on the Website. 'Hey YouTubers, it's Paris,' she said in an introductory video on her channel. 'YouTube is the hottest community on the Web and that's where I want to be. My album is out now and I want to share it with all of you. It's called Paris and I hope you love it.

'I've got my own YouTube channel and there you can see me in the recording studio for my new music video *Stars Are Blind*, even me out partying or just hanging out with my friends. So I hope you enjoy it and come see. It's hot. Enjoy the experience and send me a comment to let me know what you think about the music. And now stay tuned for my video *Stars Are Blind*. I hope you enjoy it. Bye sexy.'

Paris's channel was a hit and quickly became the 34th most-subscribed channel of all time on the service, with over 12,000 subscriptions and more than three million views.

Staying in the electronic sphere, Paris also lent her name to a game called Jewel Jam. A time-wasting puzzle game to be played on mobile phones, it was similar to the popular game Bejewelled. The inclusion of precious gems in Jewel Jam was very suitable, given Paris's backing. In the game, players remove jewels to reveal photos of Paris and Tinkerbell. According to market research company Telephia, girls are the main buyers of phone games, and the games they prefer are puzzles.

In 2006, Paris attended the Electronic Entertainment Expo to promote Jewel Jam. She not only turned up late, she also inadvertently misnamed the game as she plugged it. 'Sorry I'm late,' she told the assembled throng. 'I'm really excited to have my new video game, Diamondquest. Thank you all for coming, and you can download the game,' she said.

In 2005, up and coming British comedienne Lucy Porter had written an article that heaped abuse on Paris in the *Independent*. 'Maybe she's reading improving literature all day long and is secretly a latter-day Mother Teresa,' she sneered. Little did she know how close to the mark she was because within months, Paris was being considered for the title role in Indian film director T. Rajeevnath's movie *Mother Teresa*. A Nobel Prize winner, Mother Teresa was also voted one of *Time* magazine's most important people of the 20th century. She was admired around the world as a living saint for her work with the dispossessed and downtrodden. Some commentators questioned her canonisation in the latter years of her life but she remains a hugely revered person.

The filmmaker said a computer-generated image shows a close facial match between the Albanian-born nun and Paris. 'My agents have contacted Paris Hilton,' said the award-winning director, confirming the story. 'Although there are several actresses willing to play the role of Mother Teresa, the most widely-respected and loved person, the history of the actress who is finally chosen for the role would have to be analysed thoroughly before she is chosen.'

Apparently, what had drawn Rajeevnath to Paris was her refusal to pose nude for *Playboy* magazine. Naturally, the media had a good laugh at this unlikely development but the 65-year-old director was unabashed. 'I think she'll be a hit. The preliminary script has been readied. And the proceeds of the film would go to the Missionaries of Charity. By June this year, the groundwork for the film would be complete and I propose to begin shooting in West Bengal and several foreign countries in early 2007.'

Paris was naturally extremely flattered. 'It's such an honour. I'm so excited. I really want to learn more about this amazing woman, so that's what I'm doing in a few months.' However, she did temper her enthusiasm slightly by adding that she didn't think she and the Macedonian-born nun looked at all alike. In preparation for the role, Paris is reported to have joined the Order of Mother Teresa missionaries, and travelled around Bangalore and Calcutta. A source close to her said, 'Paris is tougher than most people think. But I don't think she knows what she's let herself in for. The Calcutta nuns are notoriously strict, so she will have to be on her best behaviour.'

The rumour mill has it that Paris lost the part after asking the director if she could meet the nun's children as part of her research. 'I think the word mother confused her,' said a friend. Or perhaps somewhere along the line another of Paris's jokes got missed. Either way, another work proposal quickly emerged from India for her. Indian-American designer Anand Jon asked Paris to model some of his creations. 'Who could be better than Paris – the ultimate It girl – to present my designs?' he beamed. 'Paris is a very close friend of mine. We have known each other for a long time… For her, India is the land of exotica and beauty. In fact, her response was "I finally get to visit the exotic!" She is a style diva. She is very particular about what she wears. She is the Madonna of our generation.'

The part in the Mother Teresa film might have ultimately eluded her but Paris was now ready to take her place in the fourth season of *The Simple Life*. However, the preparations for this season were to be far from simple. Firstly, given her falling out with Richie, Paris was insistent that her former friend would take no part in the show. She announced that instead of Nicole, her friend

Kimberly Stewart – who she had put forward for the show originally – would star alongside her. However, Fox Network head Peter Ligouri insisted that Stewart was not going to be involved, and Paris and Richie were 'TV professionals, who will be ready to work together when the time comes'.

The story became even more complicated when Fox abruptly cancelled its plans for any further seasons in October 2005, both because it had filled its mid-season show quota, and because of concerns about Paris and Richie's ability to work together. 'We're disappointed that *The Simple Life* will not continue on Fox where it has performed so well, but we believe this series starring Paris Hilton and Nicole Richie is still a dynamic and valuable franchise,' said 20th Century Fox Television's official announcement, before punting for any takers. 'We hope to be able to announce a new network partner in the coming days.'

'We have a hit series with 18- to 49-year-olds starring two of the most written about women in the world,' Jon Murray said in the company's own statement. 'We're very excited about the creative plans for the next group of episodes, and are confident this situation will be remedied quickly.' After it was dropped by Fox, other networks, including NBC, The WB, VH1 and MTV were all reported to be interested in obtaining the rights to air new seasons of the show

However, it ended up on E! Networks, a network which had been obsessed with Paris's story for so many years. E! Networks' president and CEO Ted Harbert said he was aggressive in pursuing the show, which he wanted on E! for a few reasons. 'One, E! needs a comedy; two, E! needs a high-profile show because I want to show that we are being very aggressive in programming this network; and three, Paris and Nicole are just great representatives of the E! brand – our fans love them. Whenever we do anything about them, we get ratings.' He added, '*The Simple Life* was the most expensive series E! had ever undertaken,' and said that Paris and Nicole 'both live the life of E!'.

It was then decided that the pair would appear separately in the fourth season, the filming of which finally began in February 2006. The fourth season, called *'Til Death Do Us Part*, features Paris and Nicole playing the 'wife' role to a different family every episode, in a similar manner to the hit series *Wife Swap*. The girls take turns playing house with real families, and the families then decide which of them is better in the role. Therefore, the subtext of the series was the competition between the two girls in not only the show but in life in general. In one episode, Hilton characterised her and Nicole as complete opposites. 'I'm the nice one, she's the evil one,' she said.

Once more, the show received fulsome praise from the critics, including some reluctant ones. Chris Quinn in the *San Antonio Express* wrote: *'Til Death Do Us Part* features America's favourite spoiled skeletal duo in a thoughtless, yet charming, attempt to find out and/or prove they can handle life as average wives and mothers. It is kind of like putting a brainless monkey in Washington, D.C., to see if it can function and do as good a job as any average politician. Oh wait, bad analogy.'

He went on to say that much as he fought the idea of watching this show in the beginning, he was now stuck to it every week. 'Like a junkie, or Renfield, I lurk near the TV on Sunday nights as the clock nears 9 p.m.' When the show debuted, it drew 1.3 million viewers. While those ratings would have been dismal for Fox, they were actually more than four times E!'s prime-time average and in key adult demographic groups, ratings 'more than tripled from the network's average'.

The publicity for the show declared that 'Reality television has never been this wild… Simply put, it's simply outrageous,' but in truth, this was the weakest of the first four seasons. With Paris and Richie sharing little screen time, their magic rapport was almost entirely absent. Perhaps the most memorable moment during shooting came when Richie asked an 11-year-old boy if he thought she was a 'milf'. 'I don't know what that means,' the youngster replied. At first, in fact, the boy thought she'd said 'elf'. Richie clarified, 'It means a "mother I'd like to f*ck".' This took place with two camera operators and other crew taping the exchange. 'This happened on my driveway, on my street, to my 11-year-old son,' said the boy's angry father, who asked that his family not be identified by name.

Elsewhere, the series was notable for the girls doing their part to support same-sex marriage when they visit a lesbian couple raising two teenage daughters, and another episode where they learn about the joys of motherhood including breast-feeding and nappy changing. The series ended on a cliffhanger with the girls on the brink of a confrontation.

Paris, however, was also on the brink of big things in a new sphere – the world of pop music.

13

BLINDING STARS

At the 2006 Brit Awards at Earls Court in London, Paris reportedly told her minders to let only male admirers approach her. Female admirers, it was decreed, were unwelcome because 'Paris doesn't do girls'. This naturally raised some eyebrows among the music fraternity, but Paris was ready to make the music world stand up and take even more notice later in the year when her debut album Paris was released.

A huge music lover, Paris wrote in *Confessions* that 'Madonna may be my favourite – and obviously, I've learned a lot from her. I've loved her as long as I can remember; she's my idol. I also love Blondie… Debbie Harry rules.' Other acts she lists include Pink, Matchbox Twenty, OutKast, The Neptunes, Justin Timberlake, 50 Cent, the Black Eyed Peas, Cyndi Lauper and 'anything by my Japanese friend Yoshiki'. She also enjoys relaxing to the strains of classical music. She has also enjoyed DJing and once won an award as Best Celebrity DJ at the DanceStar awards in Miami. She knocked aside the likes of Adrien Brody, Cameron Douglas, Rosanna Arquette and Danny Masterson to win.

In 2004, Paris decided to get even more involved in the music world and record her first album. She was not the first female celebrity to dip her toe into the world of pop. Kate Winslet released a single, *What If*, in 2001 and Nicole Kidman recorded a duet with Robbie Williams the same year. Kate Moss, Jordan, Caprice and Naomi Campbell have all tried their hand at pop, too. All hoped, presumably, to repeat the magic that came the way of Kylie Minogue when, as a soap actress all those years ago, she knocked on the door of Pete Waterman.

Paris took a different path to the Aussie, when she created her own label – Heiress Records. She began work the same year on her album, *Paris*. Although she was nervous at first, she quickly surprised herself once she began work in the studio. 'I have always had a voice and always known I could sing, but I was too shy to let it come out,' she said. 'I think that's the hardest thing you can do, to sing in front of people. When I finally let go and did it, I realized it is what I am most talented at and what I love to do the most.'

Not only was it fun in its own right, it also gave Paris a renewed sense of worth. 'I'm so proud of myself right now – I'm very, very proud,' she said. 'Just because my last name's Hilton and I come from this family, it doesn't mean I can't be talented or know music, or know what I'm doing. People will see – they just have to listen to the record!'

Once again, Paris was keen to prove that being rich with a famous name doesn't mean you don't have talents. Make no mistake, these were very happy days in the studio for Paris with her impressive team of songwriters and producers. 'My experience in the studio was amazing. Each producer and song came to life in various ways for each recording. I really enjoyed the process with each song and, consequently, my album is so wide in its range and expression.'

The album was released on Warner Bros. Chairman Tom Whalley says he had no doubt about signing up Paris once he'd heard her voice. 'When I realized she could sing, I knew we could make a record.' The pool of talent that was put together to make that record included top producers such as Jonathan 'JR' Rotem, Scott Storch, Dr Luke, Greg Wells and Kara DioGuardi. JR Rotem has produced for rapper The Game, Destiny's Child, Britney Spears, Snoop Dogg, Rihanna and Dr Dre. Scott Storch has worked with Busta Rhymes, Snoop Dogg, Boyz II Men, Beyonce and Janet Jackson. Dr Luke has worked with Britney Spears, Kelly Clarkson, Lady Sovereign, Avril Lavigne, Missy Elliott and Pink. Greg Wells was dubbed 'the studio Swiss Army knife' by Stewart Copeland of The Police and has also worked with a host of stars including Daniel Bedingfield. Kara DioGuardi has worked for Kylie Minogue and Natalie Imbruglia.

Naturally, this made for a very varied set of tracks, as Paris revealed while she was making the album. 'The whole album has so much different music on it. I like all music. It's not like I only like pop or only rock. I want to have something for everybody.' More and more positive reports emerged from the studio as her production team were full of praise for Paris. DioGuardi said the album was, 'Fun music. It's danceable, with elements of Blondie, a little reggae and great beats. She has a very sweet voice, very breathy. It sounds exactly like what you would want Paris to be doing.' Storch, too, was impressed. 'She's actually got quite a musical ability. Her rhythm is better than a lot of people I've recorded in the past.' Luke Gottwald, aka Dr Luke, added, 'She has a really cool tone, particularly in the lower register. So I didn't want to make a song where Paris was copying anybody else.'

Paul Oakenfold, the superstar DJ who has remixed songs for the likes of Madonna, U2 and Jennifer Lopez, admits he was initially sceptical of working with Paris when he was approached by Warner Bros executives. Then he heard *Turn It Up* and was quickly won over, as were many of those who heard him playing the track in nightclubs. 'I was surprised by how good her vocal was,' he says. 'I've gotten a good response on it. A lot of DJs who go on after me ask me who it is. I say Paris Hilton and they're really surprised.'

All this praise from serious music moguls must have been a great boost for Paris. But perhaps the sweetest music to her ears came from Jordan Juicy J. Houston. 'I was shocked that she would want to listen to one of my tracks. As far as my writing and producing abilities, winning the Oscar was number one. But number two is, wow, Paris Hilton is interested in using some of my music.'

Words say a lot but actions speak even louder and when Paris went to Miami's Winter Conference and joined Oakenfold in his DJ booth for the point in his set where he plays *Turn It Up*, she saw in front of her eyes the effect her music had on people. 'You could see the whole place was dancing,' remembers Oakenfold of the moment the song kicked in. 'She was really happy with it, the whole place was going crazy.'

It is little surprise then that during interviews at this time, Paris was full of enthusiasm about the whole project. She said, 'My music now is a top priority and I hope that everyone can recognise how hard I have worked on this album and understand that my music is so personal to me. I will be working very hard to have a tour that complements my music.'

Paris said that she had been working on this project for years and writing lyrics and songs since she was little, but 'now I have found my inner voice and with the great producers that I worked with on this album I feel I've completed the album I always dreamed of making. I think the combination of my taste, style and voice, along with the vast range of musical influences on my album, creates a sound that will leave a mark on music.

'As soon as my fans and the critics hear my album, I am sure that everyone at first will be, like, "Wow! This is really, really good!" I love all kinds of music whether it be pop, hip-hop, dance or reggae. So I felt like I can do anything. I wanted to do an eclectic mix so everyone can enjoy it. This has been a dream of mine since I was six years old.'

So just how good was the album? Paris kicks off with *Turn It Up*, a moody R&B classic that begins with Paris whispering her catchphrase 'That's hot'. Teasing and full of attitude, it's a sassy and sexy start to the album. The mood changes completely with track two, *Stars Are Blind*, which is a happy, summery, reggae-tinged tune. The album then segues into *I Want You*. Beginning with Paris's sexy cry of 'JR' – presumably a nod to the producer of the same name – it's brass-backed tune revs up the lyrics, which combine vulnerability with confidence perfectly.

Then comes one of the most talked-about tracks on the album, *Jealousy*. The mournful violin that opens the track signals a change in mood to a more sombre note, though the chorus builds to more of a tone of righteous anger. *Heartbeat* is the soundtrack to girls putting on their make-up and preparing for a night out. *Nothing In The World* is a short, sweet, hip-swinger of a tune. The same could be said of the next track, *Screwed*, although this one really rocks and is the album's main sing-a-long tune. She admits that when her parents first heard the title *Screwed*, they were less than impressed. However, once Kathy listened to it she loved it. *Not Leaving Without You* opens with some country & western slide guitar and bops along nicely. *Turn You On* sees Paris boasting that everybody's looking at her and promising to give people something to write about. It's the most Parisesque tune on the album. Then, it's a bit of fun with her cover of Rod Stewart's *Do Ya Think I'm Sexy*, which Paris makes her own.

The launch party was held at Pure nightclub inside Caesars Palace, Las Vegas. The mayor of Las Vegas mayor had proclaimed it Paris Hilton Day and presented her with a key to the city. 'I would totally stalk her,' said fan Jeff Wright outside the launch. 'Actually, I'm a really big fan. I was kind of curious to see what all the hype was about. Is Paris Hilton really the superstar she claims to be?' Inside, the guest-list included sister Nicky Hilton, film star Stormy Daniels, Jeff Beacher, singer Eric Benét, professional skateboarder Chad Muska, plus musicians Eve and Travis Barker. It was a great day for Paris; earlier on five skywriting planes had written: 'Congrats on your CD Paris' outside her penthouse suite at Caesars Palace.

When she came to Britain to promote her music, Paris came to the attention of loudmouth British comedian Russell Brand. 'Would I bonk her brains out?' he said. 'Yes of course, I'm making it a mission to meet her while she's here. There's nothing better than thinking of getting to know her type is there? She looks like butter wouldn't melt, but I want to get past that.' Paris was asked how she felt about this prospect and replied, 'Who? I think I know of him. Is he wealthy?'

Having had praise from her production team, nightclub crowds and a zany stand-up comic, what sort of reaction would Paris receive from the sharp pens of the music

critics? The *Sun* newspaper had tipped Paris to become
the new Britney Spears but many UK critics admitted that
they had been sharpening their pens and their tongues for
some time in anticipation of Paris's album. They wanted
to bury her but many found that they ended up praising
her. The *Evening Standard* raved, 'Stars Are Blind is
unashamedly terrific.' The *Sunday Star* enthused, 'Radio
friendly, a well-produced record that's as polished as the
25-year-old's nails.' Meanwhile, the *Sunday Express* spoke
of, 'A clutch of songs – *Stars Are Blind*, *I Want You* and,
especially, the brilliant *Jealousy* that elevate the pouting
heiress to true pop-star status.' Even the *Guardian* was
moved to praise: 'An appealing confection of bubblegum
pop, stomp-rock, disco and hip-hop lite.' The broadsheet
also said, '*Stars Are Blind* was actually rather brilliant – like
a cross between UB40 and Britney Spears. And the rest of
the album, while never repeating the trick, certainly isn't
any worse than recent offerings from Jessica Simpson,
Rachel Stevens or any number of other so-called "proper"
pop stars.' Meanwhile the *Daily Telegraph*'s Neil
McCormick gave somewhat equivocal and snotty praise
when he said, 'For an album by someone with no
discernible musical talent, Paris is surprisingly effective,
polished and professional. Judging by the interest her
every move has generated thus far, it will probably add
considerably to the Hilton treasure chest, simply on the
basis that it is not actually unlistenable.'

So, very healthy praise from the UK critics but in
America, the response was often even warmer. One of

the earliest and most perceptive responses came from *Blender* magazine. Editor-in-chief Craig Marks hit the nail on the head when he said, 'It's a record for her to dance on banquettes to. Not a sit down and analyze the lyrics type of record. And it's not Mariah Carey; this is the touchstone of a generation type of record. And it's not intended to be – any more than a chick-lit book intends to win a Pulitzer Prize.' The *Village Voice* echoed Blender's review. 'It doesn't delve into topics any more profound than dancing on tables, backstabbing, and trashing around, it's exactly what you'd want from a slumming socialite's CD, and it's more fun than blowing Bazooka bubbles at Anna Wintour.'

Writing in the *Boston Herald*, Jed Gottlieb put the cat among the pigeons when he compared Paris to the debuts of pop royalty. 'It's actually got more potential hits than Christina's or Britney's first efforts,' he gushed. 'And it shows she's got plenty of blonde ambition. But her fate rests on whether America wants to embrace its guiltiest pleasure as its sexiest pop star. My guess? Sure, we'll love our sighing, singing Paris – at least until something sexier comes along 15 minutes later.' Randy Lewis, in *Los Angeles Times*, was scarcely less impressed. 'The cheap shot going around about the breathless musical debut of Paris, Pop Star, is that with the likes of producers and songwriters Scott Storch, Kara DioGuardi and J.R. Rotem at the helm, your grandmother could get a hit single. But after an honest listen to the 11 songs on her dance-minded album, the reality – and the house of Paris is built on reality, albeit reality TV and videotape – is "Book that studio, Granny!"'

People magazine said: '*Turn It Up*, one of five songs that Hilton co-wrote, is a sexy, Britney-esque thumper made to be pumped in the strip club, while the single *Stars Are Blind* has a reggae-pop shimmer that makes for frothy summer fun.' Elsewhere, reviews included the following: 'The heiress has made the album you'd expect, but it's executed better than you would imagine. Madonna has recorded worse CDs.' (*St Louis Post Dispatch*); 'It's not likely to be forgotten.' (*Hartford Courant*); '*Stars Are Blind* is the perfect shtick for the socialite-turned-singer's dumb-blonde persona.' (*Sunday Telegram*); 'Hilton delivers.' (*Home News Tribune*). As for the music establishment, the *All Music Guide* said, 'Make no mistake, *Paris* is a very good pop album, at times deliberately reminiscent of Blondie, Madonna, and Gwen Stefani, yet having its own distinct character – namely, Paris's persona, which is shamelessly shallow and devoid of any depth.'

So, plenty of praise from the critics but how would Paris's music fare once it went on sale? There had been plenty of excitement about the album since Fox News revealed the track-list in March 2006. Paris went head-to-head in a summer battle with fellow platinum blonde Christina Aguilera. Not that Paris was intimidated by this. 'Not at all,' she insisted. 'We have the same management and I often hang out with Christina. She's really sweet. I'm going to buy her album. We like talking about fashion, what's going on in our lives and guys. People are surprised I can sing and I think. "What's the big deal?" It is a little insulting, but I love to surprise people.'

Once released, Paris debuted at number 6 on the Billboard 200 and the single *Stars Are Blind* peaked at 18 on the Billboard Hot 100. It reached number four in Canada. *Stars Are Blind* became the most requested single on radio stations in Los Angeles and New York during June and it became, at the same time, one of the most downloaded songs on iTunes. It reached number one in a number of countries including Belgium and Hungary. Paris is very proud of her album. 'I still cry when I play my CD in the car or at home because it's so good.'

Although *Stars Are Blind* – the video for which was filmed in May 2006 in Malibu – was a favourite for many reviewers, much of the media's attention also focused on *Jealousy*, which it was widely believed was a message to Nicole Richie.

'It's a song about any girl who has a girlfriend that's jealous of you,' said Paris. 'It's about someone being mean and evil. Nicole and I are not enemies, but I can't be friends with someone who doesn't want good things for me. I'm the nicest, most loyal person in the world when it comes to my friends. I would really do almost anything to make sure they're happy. But I only want friends who are there for me just like I'm there for them. Otherwise it's too painful. I brought Nicole on to *The Simple Life*, and all of a sudden she became this different person. She dropped her old friends and she's someone else.'

While promoting her album in the UK, she made all

the right noises when she gave generous praise to the domestic music scene. 'I'd love to perform here next year,' she said. 'That would be hot. I really like James Blunt and Robbie Williams and Keane. Arctic Monkeys are cool. I think they can break the US. If they come out to LA when I'm there I'd take them to Hyde. It's a rock and roll bar. They let in only 50 people so it's the place to go. And there's no cameras.'

In April 2007, Paris, Lindsay Lohan and Kimberly Stewart were seen chatting with Arctic Monkeys at a party hosted by GQ magazine at LA's Viceroy hotel during the Coachella Festival. They then headed to a party at Frank Sinatra's house. As we'll see, Paris's name would also soon be sharing headlines with both James Blunt and Robbie Williams.

Not that every Brit reciprocated her love. In September 2006 it was revealed that 'guerrilla graffiti artist' Banksy had secretly smuggled 500 doctored copies of her album into record stores. Featuring their own cover art and sarcastic song titles such as *Why Am I Famous?*, *What Have I Done?* and *What Am I For?* the cover art featured Paris topless or with a dog's head. It was a silly protest from a silly man. Banksy has been accused of hypocrisy by many for the way he combines his anti-capitalist stance with work for major companies, and for selling his 'art' for big bucks at establishment auctioneers Sotheby's. Among his attention-seeking stunts have been covering live animals in paint and visiting the Middle East to paint on Israel's security wall; in doing so he managed to offend a number of Israelis and Palestinians and returned home with his tail between his legs.

For someone who claims to be so edgy, it was surprising that Banksy turned on Paris. His spokeswoman Jo Brooks did little to dispel the confusion. 'He's saying you can be a celebrity, but you don't have to do music. I don't know what the reaction will be in America or whether she would even get it. We wanted it to stay underground as long as possible. But it's gone a little bit *Charlie And The Chocolate Factory* now. Everyone wants one.' Perhaps the most telling aspects of the protest were the inclusion of the doctored topless image – sexual frustration or jealousy on Banksy's part? – and his mocking song title, *What Have I Done?* Well, Banksy, what she had done was start several successful companies, release an album, write a bestselling book, and star on a successful reality television series and in a series of films. Next to all that, what have you done?

There was quickly another entry to add to Paris's CV, to once more prove Banksy and her other critics wrong. Directed by Erik MacArthur, *Bottoms Up* is a comedy that sends up Hollywood society in much the same way that *Zoolander* sent up the fashion world. In the film that is described as being in the same vein as *Swingers*, Paris starred alongside Jason Mewes (made famous in *Clerks II*, *Dogma*) and Brian Hallisay in the film that bills itself as 'one sexy, scandalous comedy "that's hot" but goes down smooth'. It received praise even among the notoriously harsh reviewers at IMDb, who managed to be positive about the film and Paris's role in it. 'All the actors including Hilton do deliver some strong scenes,' wrote one reviewer. 'Had the movie been put in the hands of an indie filmmaker who is used to no money, or if a few more million were thrown at it, it would have turned out to be a good long-lasting flick.'

Entertainment Weekly wrote: 'It is funnier than its title. Mewes is a Minnesota bartender who heads to Hollywood to save his father's steak house and ends up blackmailing a studio head's daughter (Hilton) and exploiting her "It" boyfriend (a Josh Duhamel-like Brian Hallisay) with the help of a gay uncle (scene-stealer Keith, doing his best Rip Taylor). While Mewes shows surprising depth sans his mentor, director Kevin Smith (who cameos), new pop star Hilton goes brunette.'

Former Bond girl and stunning model Catherine McQueen had a ball working alongside Paris in *Bottoms Up*. 'Making it was an absolute hoot,' she recalls. 'It's about the Los Angeles party scene so in that respect the whole thing is pretty much sex, drugs and rock'n'roll. Paris plays this crazy 'It' girl who is juggling a couple of boyfriends and I'm one of her party animal friends. It was fantastic because we were shooting scenes in all the top LA nightclubs and at this mad mansion in Beverly Hills.'

According to McQueen it was a riot from start to finish. 'I imagined Paris would be very snooty and a bit of a nightmare to be around but just the opposite was true. She's lovely – but definitely a bit on the kooky side. She had everyone tearing their hair out because she would spend all day getting her make-up done for a scene. Then she would ruin it all before the cameras got rolling by having a butler bring her big trays of burgers and hotdogs.

'I don't think she quite realised how much hassle this was causing everyone, but she seems to be on a different planet half the time. At the time there were all these rumours flying around that Paris was pregnant and I thought the junk food diet was maybe her having cravings. But Paris just laughed off the baby rumours and told me she just likes to eat rubbish all the time. I don't know how she manages to scoff all that stuff and still be built like a pipe-cleaner. I have to work out in the gym for hours every day just to keep trim.' Paris later admitted, however, that she had put in a lot of work in at the gym in the build up to the filming.

But not everybody was so enthusiastic about working alongside Paris. There were less than glowing words for her from another of her co-stars, Simona Fusco. 'My biggest problem with Paris was that she was always late on the set,' she moaned. 'It became very annoying. Everyone gets tired. By the time Paris finally showed up she was usually coming from a party. It was a very long day working with Paris.'

Shirley MacLaine emerged from the doldrums of retirement at this point to hurl abuse at Paris. 'So she wears pink and has blonde hair and suddenly she calls herself not a starlet or an ingenue – no, according to Paris she is a movie star! It irritates me as in my day you had to really work. It took Bette Davis seven years of hard slog to reach the point where her name was above the title on a movie.' Ooh, get her!

Well, as MacLaine was putting her claws away, Paris's name appeared above the title in another movie. She was first attracted to *Pledge This!* because it came from the National Lampoon stable, which was also the source of the legendary film *Animal House* – a favourite of Paris's. She began shooting the film in the autumn of 2004 and it was released in 2006.

In the film Paris plays Victoria English, the president of the hottest college sorority in the US at the South Beach University in Miami, Florida. She has just one dream – to be featured on the front cover of *FHM* magazine. Described as 'glamorous, sexy and viciously ambitious', Victoria is as determined and focussed as the person that plays her. Her director William Heins was kinder than the likes of MacLaine when he said, 'She is a star, but she'll be a respected actor in no time.'

Paris attended the world premiere of the film in Chicago and as usual a crowd of fans turned up to catch a glimpse of her. 'She won't be able to dress as skimpy in this weather as she does in California,' said one Paris fan. Another added, 'I love that Paris doesn't care what people think about her and that she does what she wants.' She arrived fashionably late wearing sunglasses, a black coat and knee-high grey boots. She waved to her fans and signed autographs. 'I love Chicago. It's cool to be here,' she beamed.

While promoting the film in Cannes, Paris seemed to be

finding it cool to be there too. An onlooker said, 'She and her pals started drinking on a yacht at 6 p.m. Then they moved on to a few other swish drinking holes. By 2.30 a.m. they were still up for a party so they headed to the Hotel du Cap, where Hollywood stars such as Val Kilmer are staying.' But despite all the partying, Paris somehow managed to look her usual stunning self the next day at a photo shoot on the pier of the Carlton Hotel.

Shortly after her album had been released in the UK, Paris attended a charity event in Los Angeles. Afterwards, as she drove her £300,000 Mercedes-Benz SLR McLaren through Hollywood in the early hours of the morning, she was pulled over by police. An LAPD spokesman said, 'The officers observed that Hilton exhibited the symptoms of intoxication. A sobriety test was conducted and the officers determined she was driving under the influence.' She had to say a swift goodbye to Kimberly Stewart, who was the passenger in the car. She was then handcuffed and led away. At 2 a.m., still wearing her white designer dress, diamond jewellery and full make-up, she was released into the arms of sister Nicky and her boyfriend Kevin Connolly.

On Thursday morning, Paris called in to Ryan Seacrest's *On Air* radio show to explain what had happened. 'You know what – it was nothing,' she said. 'I'd been shooting my music video for my new song, *Nothing In This World*. I got off last night at about 10 p.m. then I went and had dinner with my sister and all my girlfriends, and then we went to this charity event Dave Navarro threw for brain tumours. And, um, I had one margarita, starving 'cause I had not eaten all day, on my way to In-N-Out, which is probably three blocks away, and I'm in my SLR, which is a little fast, so maybe I was speeding a little bit, and I got pulled over.' Seacrest asked if she was driving erratically, as reported. 'No. I was just really hungry and I wanted to have an In-N-Out burger!' She added, 'There was a lot of paparazzi around, so I think they were trying to make a statement.'

Her alcohol level was 0.8 per cent – just over the limit. Spokesman Elliot Mintz explained that the reading was caused by 'one drink on an empty stomach after a full day's work'. He added, 'She was literally the minimum over the limit that you would need to be to warrant being pulled over. She is taking this seriously.' Paris herself said, 'I was starving because I had not eaten all day. My SLR is pretty fast, so maybe I was speeding a little bit and I got pulled over.' Inevitably, another setback in Paris's life led to the normal round of 'is this the end of Paris?' speculation. Mintz tried his best to throw water over the story. 'The people who enjoy Paris as a comedian or actress on TV or as a singer on her CD, a woman who seems to have captured the imagination of so many people, I don't know if this is going to have any impact on them one way or another.' Both Mintz and Paris might have done their best to play the incident down but it would prove to be the catalyst for a series of events that would lead to Paris facing a painful fate.

The next time she was seen in public she was wearing a black wig and hat in an attempt to keep a low profile. However, she was recognised by photographers and reporters who fired questions at her. Within days, she attended the 21st birthday bash of Sam Branson, son of Virgin tycoon Sir Richard, who set up a practical joke at Paris's expense at the party. The £150,000 party, held at Sir Richard's Oxfordshire estate, was a mad-hatter themed event and when Sir Richard discovered that Paris planned to arrive dressed as Alice in Wonderland he quietly ordered all 60 waitresses to also dress as Alice, thus humiliating Paris. He went one stage further by asking Paris to fetch him a drink when she arrived.

Then she returned to the US for New York Fashion week where she was seen looking tired at the Jovovich-Hawke show. Soon after this, she was out shopping on Robertson Boulevard, LA, when a female fan approached her for a chat. 'Paris seemed really sad and tried to explain that she was in a rush,' said an onlooker. 'When the young girl asked if everything was OK, Paris shook her head before fleeing in tears.' This turned out to be because she had just received the news – which broke the following day – that she had been charged for drink driving following her arrest in Hollywood. 'The charges are consistent with California law and the circumstances of this case,' said Nick Velasquez, a spokesman for city prosecutors.

The press were quick to claim that 'Paris could face jail'. However, this was not at the time considered a likely outcome as first-time offenders are nearly always given probation. Sure enough, when her case went to court in January 2007, Paris was not jailed. She admitted reckless driving in a deal with prosecutors after she was charged with being over the limit behind the wheel, which she denied. Her plea went in via her lawyers, as she did not attend the hearing. The court gave her 36 months' probation, a £582 fine, and ordered her to attend a drink education programme. Judge Michael Sauer also imposed other conditions. 'The city attorney believes that this is a fair disposition to this case,' said Assistant City Attorney Ellen Sarmiento. 'Paris told me that she was happy the matter is over,' said Mintz. 'I just spoke with Paris an hour ago, and she's happy the matter is behind her.' And yet, within months a pair of errors of judgement would bring the matter back to life for Paris.

In the December issue of *Seventeen* magazine, Paris appeared in a public information advertisement, warning against the dangers of drink driving. 'All it takes is one drink to mess with the way you drive – it clouds your judgment and slows your reflexes. Don't take any chances,' Paris said in the ad. It was soon suggested that three months before her arrest, Paris had been involved in another motoring incident when her Range Rover backed into a car in car park after a shopping trip. The incident was allegedly caught on video. Entertainment Website TMZ posted footage of the incident on their site. Paris drove into a parked Honda Civic. The footage on TMZ.com showed her getting into her vehicle, saying goodbye to someone and then reversing. The sound of a crash can be heard. The Range Rover stops briefly and then leaves the car park. The video shows scrapes on the bumpers of both vehicles.

'Did she commit a crime? No,' Mintz said, as he once more faced a media storm on behalf of Paris. 'She was swarmed by paparazzi,' he added. 'The intensity of the lights, flashbulbs, momentarily disoriented her. She backed up, there was a minor fender-bender. No injuries. She then told me she told one of the parking people at the facility how to contact her and asked the person to please pass that along to the owner of the struck car. She did the correct thing and she would not leave the scene of a crime.'

Paris might have done the right thing in that instance but she soon made two fatal errors in driving incidents and was forced to pay a price for her actions. In the meantime, there were two successive, similar high-profile romances for Paris to enjoy.

14

IT'S ALL GREEK TO HER

Women everywhere dream of a man with the body of a Greek god – but once again, Paris lives the dream. For her, not just any old Greek hunk will do; he has to be a rich Greek heir. And not satisfied with dating one such man, she has managed to do it twice, and, as if that wasn't impressive enough, one of them shared the same first name as her!

When she spoke about the relationship with Paris Latsis in 2005, Paris Hilton pointed out that she had actually first met him many years before. 'He's not American. He's Greek. He's very loyal, the most loyal man I've ever had in my life. He's so nice and sweet and treats me like a princess. We met about eight years ago in the south of France and didn't see each other again until this year. So it's kind of like fate brought us back together.'

The two first met at Jimmy's nightclub in Monte Carlo

when they were teenagers. 'He was 14 and I was 16,' she said. 'I had this fake tattoo on my back, and he came up and was like, "Is that real?" and I totally lied and said, "Yeah." He's like, "That's hot," and I'm like, "I know." Then he said, "My name's Paris," and I said, "My name's Paris." Then we danced all night.'

Their paths did not cross again until December 2004 during a party at his mansion in Beverley Hills. 'Someone said it was Paris's party. So I was like "Who is Paris?"' recalls our Paris. 'Someone is using my name to make this party cool.' She eventually found him and they recognised each other straight away. They were inseparable right away and spent many a night together, although Paris insists that nothing physical happened between the pair for at least a month after reuniting.

So who is Paris Lastis? Born 8 August 1979, Paris Kasidokostas – to use the name he was born with – is a Greek shipping heir. The grandson of Greek shipping tycoon Yiannis Latsis who died in 2003, Paris Latsis – as he prefers to be known – is set to inherit a sizeable chunk of his late grandfather's multi-billion dollar fortune, which was made through shipping, oil and banking. Forbes listed the Latsis family in their top 100 list of the world's richest families. He is one of nine grandchildren who will share the £4 billion fortune. Paris, therefore, did not have to worry that he was after her for her money. Indeed, she has said this was the first time in her life that she felt this was the case.

Although he came from very wealthy stock, his parents

— Latsis's daughter Marianna, and Grigoris Kasidokostas — divorced when he was a young boy. He insists that they were perfect parents to him and gave him a great perspective on the world. 'My parents really took good care of me, and each one of them had to offer totally different things, because they came from different backgrounds,' he says. 'It allowed me to experience two different worlds and understand the advantages and disadvantages of coming from money.'

Paris was a fan of her new man's parents, too. She spent a Christmas vacation with them and was full of praise. She seemed so content with Latsis. 'I'm so happy. It's cool. I feel, like, really safe now, and he's just amazing. I don't even think he's real. Every day, I'm like "This is not real". I thought I was just going to settle and end up with some jackass.' He was equally as gushing about her. 'I really admire what she does,' he beamed. 'She does not achieve that from partying. She is gifted, she is talented, she can sing, she can act. It's really tough to work so hard at this age, especially for a girl that would have the option not to do it. She makes me feel that she really loves me for who I am and not for anything else. She is my soul mate, my best friend. She is the world to me.'

He was also, despite being an heir to a fortune, lower-profile than many of her previous lovers like DiCaprio, Carter and Shaw. He was very keen to keep it that way. 'Magazines want to write about the name everybody knows, but I never changed my name, because I'm low-key. It's good to have a name that people don't know.'

Hilton agreed with that. 'It's good to have a name that people don't know. I can't even pronounce that shit.' Indeed, Latsis uses his mother's maiden name because his parents are divorced and his dad's surname is quite complicated to pronounce. 'It usually gets people tongue-tied,' said a friend of his choice of surname.

Paris stepped up security for her and her man. 'I have so much surveillance and I have the best security systems. I have my guard dog and I have three security guards always outside my house.' But the guards weren't there when the paparazzi chased her down a one-way street. 'I was driving home and I drove up the wrong street and they tried to trap me in the middle of a dead end. I started screaming, it was so scary,' Paris said.

Nevertheless, life with Latsis left her contented, and the way she was behaving and speaking suggested that Paris was truly settling down. 'Now that I'm with Paris I'm really becoming a stronger person. I've just weeded out all of my friends, which is sad, but when I really think about it, the people I was hanging out with before were bad people and were using me. Now I have a couple of close friends and they really love me, they really trust me and I trust them.'

This was the most happy and content that Paris had seemed with a man since her relationship with Jason Shaw. Naturally, the media quickly started speculating feverishly that she and Latsis had become engaged. At a barbeque, a guest said, 'Whenever she would pass by, she would yell, "Hey, fiancé" [to Latsis] and he would answer back, "Yes, fiancée"!' It was very cute and coy behaviour. Eventually, the story broke that they had got engaged. He proposed to her five months after they met at his party, in the same spot where they had been reunited. He presented her with a £2.4 million ring. She said yes and moved into his mansion. In a sweet gesture he filled it with posters of her from one of her fashion campaigns for Guess. Could it be that Paris was finally going to find true, lasting love?

'He is the man I want to have my children with,' she announced. 'Paris writes me love letters and sends me roses every day. We live together and I'm very in love. He's the one. I want to have kids in the next two years, because I know that completes your life. I think having kids will make me happier than I already am. And I treat my three puppies like kids.'

Paris's statements were full of a new-found confidence as she appeared to have a new handle on herself, her image and her lifestyle. 'I thought it was cute to play a dumb blonde. On TV, I do it because it's funny. I consider myself a businesswoman and a brand. I don't enjoy going out any more. It's such a pain. It's everyone saying, "Let's do a deal! Can I have a picture?" I'm just, like, these people are such losers. I can't believe I used to love doing this.'

Both sets of parents were very happy with the relationship. 'He is a wonderful young man,' said Kathy. 'We love him. If he didn't ask our permission, I'd be very angry. My husband would be furious.' Meanwhile, Latsis's father said, 'Paris is a very beautiful girl. I love Paris like a daughter [when I met her] I understood why my son is so crazy about her.' He added. 'When you're in love, everything's beautiful, especially the woman in your life. When I was in love, I turned the world upside down. And then I put it back again.' His mother was less keen, according to a family friend. 'She doesn't think this will end in marriage. Partly, she thinks her son is too young. But also it's all the publicity. If Hilton were a normal girl, without the publicity, it would be fine. If she were a Hilton, without the publicity, that would be fine. But the Latsis family hate publicity.'

It was time for the two families to meet to celebrate the engagement. As the two families prepared for the summit, they had to face plenty of publicity. The *Evening Standard* dispatched a journalist to Mykonos to cover the countdown to the big meeting between two families who between them were worth billions of pounds. 'This is where the parents of Paris Hilton, 24, and her fiancé Paris Kasidokostas (known to the world's press by his mother's surname of Latsis), 26, are meeting,' wrote Charlotte Eagar. 'The island of Mykonos, where Greek society goes to play, is electrified with gossip, for the encounter promises to be a tense one. On his side are his mother, Marianna Latsis, the Princess Royal of a £4.5 billion Greek shipping fortune and doyenne of the Greek intelligentsia, and her lover of many years, Nikos Kourkoulos, a Seventies film star and Greek heartthrob, now chairman of the National Theatre of Greece. On hers are Kathy and Rick Hilton, third generation of the hotel dynasty founded by Conrad Hilton, who was born in New Mexico in 1887 and died in 1979. Forbes magazine estimates the family's worth at about £150 million.'

The locals were as excited as the journalist about this billionaire family get-together. 'Everybody is talking about it here,' said one party girl on Mykonos beach. 'They can't talk about anything else. Have you seen them? Where are they?' Of course, it had not escaped anyone's attention that Paris and her fiancé shared the same Christian name. Some saw this as the ultimate narcissism; as for Paris herself she just found the coincidence a bit of fun. Asked what they would name their children if they had any, her answer was, 'Paris, Paris, Paris, Paris.' As well as nicknaming each other 'fiancé' at the barbeque party, they had other cute nicknames for one another. He called her Princess and she called him Babaluna.

With her new-found confidence, came a more mature self-image in Paris, and a more homely lifestyle. She was keen to point out the diversion between the highly sexual imagery of her photo shoots, music videos and television advertisements and the real Paris Hilton, who loved nothing more than to stay home with her beloved fiancé. 'I think I'm sexual in pictures and the way I dress and my whole image but at home I'm really not like that. I'd rather sit in bed and watch TV. All of my ex-boyfriends – of course, not Paris – would be like "What's the problem? You're so not sexual!"'

Nevertheless, with an eye on their plans for marriage,

Paris was looking far away from home for the ceremony. 'I've always wanted to be a princess on my big day and only a wedding in England could make that happen,' she revealed. She added that if 'Prince Charles got married in St Paul's' then it was good enough for her. After all, she believes she is the closest thing to American royalty. She also planned to buy a home in London for her and Latsis. The couple once stopped off in London on their way to Greece. They were spotted looking cosy at the Serpentine Gallery party, at the Live 8 concert, and at Kabaret's nightclub in Beak Street. The Serpentine bash was, incidentally, voted one of the Top 10 parties of the year by the *Evening Standard ES* magazine and Paris's attendance was given as one of the major reasons. At Boujis, in South Kensington, they looked more hot than cosy. 'She had her skirt hitched up and was grinding back and forth on his lap. It was so obvious that they wanted people to watch,' said an interested onlooker. With new confidence, a mega-flash engagement ring on her finger and plans afoot for a grand wedding, things looked rosy for Paris.

When the pair holidayed in St Tropez, Latsis showed he was prepared to defend the honour of his fiancée. He thumped a young German guy who was trying to chat up Paris in an exclusive club at the Hotel Byblos. He removed a tattoo he had of an ex-girlfriend, thus consigning to history his relationship with actress Zeta Graff. Then, when Paris was spotted buying a pregnancy kit, rumours inevitably started that she was expecting his baby.

However, just five months after they got engaged, their relationship was over. Paris released a statement saying: 'I'm sad to announce that I've called off my engagement. Over the last couple of months I've realized that this is the right decision for me. We remain best of friends, and I'll always love him. I hope people will respect my privacy during this emotional time.' She added, 'I have seen the break-ups between people who love each other and rush into getting married too quickly. I do not want to make that mistake. I'm still young and still have a very active career that I'm not prepared to give up. I have worked very hard to get to where I am. Paris is a great guy and we will handle this with dignity and respect.' She later said, 'I'm still young and I have a very active career that I'm not prepared to give up. I've worked very hard to get where I am.'

'She didn't want to make a mistake with the whole world watching,' said her aunt, Kyle Richards. 'When Paris gets married she wants it to be forever.' What brought their relationship to an end? Various theories were aired. One was from a friend who said that Paris had come to realise that her and Latsis were 'very different people'. She hoped that if she stuck it out that this might become less of an issue. It didn't, said the friend, so Paris decided to move on. Another source said that the couple 'have been at one another's throats … they have gone from being head over heels in love to fighting. It's really upsetting her. It is mostly over silly things but it's having a really bad affect on their relationship.'

Others claim that Latsis's mother hit the roof when she found out about Paris's sex-tape scandal. As we've seen, she was less than excited by the relationship from the start. 'She was frankly disgusted and had to make her feelings known to her son,' claimed a source close to the Greek family. 'She told him he is making the family a laughing stock. And she told her son that for the sake of the family's honour he must never marry Paris. She told him to get rid of her now.' Certainly, Paris subsequently revised her initial gushing comment about the time she met Latsis's parents. 'They asked me lots of questions about culture and stuff that no one my age could be expected to know,' she complained.

Even before the split, Latsis's parents were pouring cold water over the plans. 'I know that she says she wants to get married to [my son] Paris, but that doesn't mean this will happen tomorrow,' said his father, backtracking somewhat on his initial praising tone for Paris. 'My opinion, as well as his mother's, is that he is too young and he should wait.' On reports that his son was showering Paris with expensive jewellery, he snapped, 'He knows that it would be more useful to give this money ... to an orphanage or people who suffer from something, rather than buying these kinds of gifts.' Once the split was announced, the parents were said to be over the moon.

Whatever the reasons for the split, the truth was that Paris's hopes that she had finally found true, lasting love had again been dashed. She kept the famous engagement ring because when she offered to return it to her former fiancé, he said he was keen for her to keep hold of it. 'Right now is a very tough time for me,' he said in a statement. 'I love Paris very much. This was the best experience of my life.'

Days after the split, she was seen dancing all night at the Palms Casino in Las Vegas with the owner George Maloof. Then she travelled to London, where during a night of hectic partying, she met Charlotte Church's ex-boyfriend, model Steven Johnson. A friend of Johnson's revealed, 'He was in the West End with friends and had the girls flocking around him as usual. But the one he ended up spending most of the night with was Paris Hilton. She was pretty smitten. There was a lot of flirting and kissing. Steve charmed her. They were very passionate with each other and swapped numbers.

'They've been in contact ever since by mobile and things have been getting very steamy. Steve is pretty blown away by it all and thinks it could be the real thing. He really likes her but wants to keep it all under wraps. He isn't saying too much at the moment so we'll have to wait and see what happens.'

What happened was that she quickly forgot about Johnson and instead transferred her sights to another Greek shipping heir, Stavros Niarchos III. In October they were regularly seen clubbing together in venues across LA, and dining at a Japanese restaurant in West Hollywood. Stavros Niarchos was born in New York on 17 April 1985 but grew up in the French city of – yeah, you guessed it – Paris. He is the eldest son of Philip

Niarchos, who inherited a sizable share of his father's shipping business, and his third wife Victoria Guinness, who is heir to the fortune of the beer company. He studied film at the University of Southern California and is a passionate kiteboarder – which involves riding a small surfboard while being pulled by a kite. The Niarchos family fortune has been estimated at over £1 billion.

In the past, Niarchos had dated actress Mary-Kate Olsen. In dating high-profile women, he was continuing the tradition set by his grandfather who – as a lifelong rival of Aristotle Onassis – married his rival's ex-wife Tina and also once wed Henry Ford's granddaughter Charlotte Ford. Despite this, Niarchos preferred whenever possible to shun publicity – until he met Paris of course. This took place at the Spider Club in Hollywood. The next night, he joined Hilton, sister Nicky and their entourage for dinner at the Lodge before meeting up later at hotspot Element. At the club they 'danced and did shots of tequila all night long,' says an observer. 'They were all cuddled up. They kissed. She was totally happy.' However, she was also totally insistent that she and Niarchos were just good friends. 'I hang out with a lot of guy friends,' said Paris. 'I'm just having fun right now. I don't have time for a relationship.'

And what fun they were having! He sent Paris an eight-foot high bouquet for Valentine's Day. They jetted to Mexico where they romped on the beach, rode beach buggies and splashed around in the sea. They spent Christmas in Hawaii. Occasionally, the fun got a little out of control, like when a pillow fight at the Hard Rock Hotel in Las Vegas led to chaos. In his ninth-floor room, Niarchos accidentally set off some fire alarms, which triggered sprinklers and an evacuation of the hotel. His minder reportedly told hotel bosses, 'Why are you so upset? It's all going to be paid for.'

Paris was not part of the horseplay as she was upstairs partying with friend Kelly Osbourne, whose 21st birthday it was. The birthday girl was not overjoyed by Niarchos's behaviour. 'Paris's stupid boyfriend ruined my 21st birthday,' she railed. 'He trashed a hotel room, causing £60,000 worth of damage, and the hotel had to be evacuated. It's so unfair. The manager tried to make me pay for it, but I was having none of it. I said no bloody way because I didn't do it. Stavros caused the damage, so he can pay.' However angry she was with Niarchos, Osbourne admitted that she was not about to remove him from her social circle. 'Him and Paris are madly in love, so there's nothing I can do about it.'

Another moment of partying that went wrong for Niarchos happened when he crashed a £135,000 Bentley as he and Paris left a Hollywood nightclub. Witnesses said Stavros and Paris were in the car with two friends. 'Stavros was trying to drive while covering his face with a jacket. Unfortunately, it didn't work and he ended up hitting a parked car,' a witness said. Given what was in store for Paris in a Los Angeles court in May 2007, this incident seems somewhat chilling.

Soon, it was speculated in the press that Paris had got

engaged to her new man. 'Stavros asked her last week and she said yes straight away,' a source told the *News Of The World*. They are completely smitten. People have commented that it has all happened quickly but they have known one another for ages so they don't feel it's that much of a big deal.' This time, it seemed that the speculation was just that because all seemed far from well in their relationship. It seems the final straw came when Paris was with Niarchos and a Greek friend of his at the Hollywood Roosevelt. The two men spoke in Greek and were laughing a lot. Paris was scared that she was the object of their amusement and when he didn't seem to care, she was deeply hurt.

Only weeks earlier, she had thrown a surprise 21st birthday for her boyfriend. The couple seemed to be blissfully in love but now the relationship was over. In May 2006, her spokesman Elliot Mintz was asked whether it was true that the pair had split. He said, 'It is not my policy to comment on my client's private life. But I would not offer a denial.' Since then, there have been reports that Paris and Niarchos have got back together. In July 2006, she told People.com, 'We're together now here. We love each other.' Then they were said to be apart again. 'He gets jealous, so they argue,' a source said. 'I'm not sure if the split is permanent, but they have not been seeing each other for the past couple of weeks.'

In the same month, Paris announced that in an attempt to 'rediscover herself' she was banning all sexual activity for a year. 'I'm doing it just because I want to. I feel I'm becoming stronger as a person. Every time I have a boyfriend, I'm just so romantic, and I'll put all my energy into the guy, and I don't really pay attention to myself. One-night stands are not for me. I think it's gross when you just give it up. Guys want you more if you don't just hand it to them on a platter. If they want you, then they will wait. You have to make them work for it. I think that's the only way you know if they really want you or just want to be able to brag that they've been with you.' Then in January of the following year, a source close to Paris said of her and Niarchos, 'Everyone thought they were dunzo but Paris and Stavros are clearly still hot for each other, they really are.'

The most recent word on it came in January 2007 from yet another source close to Paris who told reporters, 'Paris dumped Stavros. She's been getting tired of him for a while. She feels he's just too insecure and immature … Stavros was devastated. He's really bummed out. He was crazy about Paris. Paris says she really cares about him as a friend, but she doesn't want to be in a relationship right now. She loves him, but she's not in love with him.'

Nonetheless, as the coming months would show, the public were still very much in love with Paris.

15

AUSSIES AND AUSTRIANS

Paris spent the Christmas season of 2006 relaxing on Australia's Bondi Beach where she was snapped wearing an extravagant Louis Vuitton bikini and noshing at the Iceburg restaurant. She was 'down under' to help promote a new low-carb beer called Bondi Blonde – truly a case of the blonde leading the blonde. The gig came about when she told her manager she wished to spend New Years' Eve in Sydney, Australia, and asked him if there was any work he could get her while she was out there. There was, and she pocketed a fee estimated at being around £2 million for the beer promotion. The drinks are on her, then!

For the brewery this was money well spent. Consumers are, it is said, becoming immune to standard, traditional advertising so getting a celebrity like Paris to endorse a product is the way forward. 'The PR campaign and editorial we got from Paris Hilton is translating into immediate sales; whereas with advertising, you're guaranteed your message is communicated as you want it, and you can control it, but whether it has any impact is another question,' said Antonia O'Neill who worked on the beer promotion.

The local mayor was equally enthused by her visit. 'Make no mistake, Paris Hilton will draw the attention of millions of people around the world to Bondi. That's good news for tourism and local business. I have to say that Paris is welcome at Bondi anytime,' George Newhouse raved. Wearing large white sunglasses, Paris told the crowds, 'Hey Australia, I'm really excited to be here.' She was a judge on a contest to pick a local model to promote the beer. Nice work if you can get it.

The year 2007 started for Paris the only way it could – with her declining the chance to endorse a Paris Hilton blow-up sex doll. 'I turn down perverted things,' she smiled. 'Like a Paris Hilton blow-up doll … They were like, "They'll sell for $50,000 each, it'll be the real-life you." And I'm like, "I really don't want a real-life me with anyone, anywhere. No!"'

This was hardly a high point for Paris but she was about to encounter a whole new low. On Tuesday 23 January, a new Website was launched with the address parisexposed.com. It claimed to have a host of private possessions of Paris including photographs, home videos, diaries, love letters, recorded phone conversations and phone numbers of friends and celebrities. Users were asked to pay a monthly fee of $39.97 to gain access to the site. The Website received 1.2 million visitors in just over 40 hours. With the sex video of her and Rick Salomon not exactly consigned to the past but certainly put in perspective by her many subsequent achievements, this invasion into her privacy must have come as a terrible shock to Paris. 'We certainly are going to explore all of our legal options about this matter,' Elliot Mintz said.

The option they took was to file a federal lawsuit against the site owners, demanding that the site be closed down. Paris's lawyer Gregory Korn said that unscrupulous individuals could use some of the site's content, including credit card receipts and her passport, 'to steal Hilton's identity, or even worse, to stalk and even physically harm Hilton.' In her lawsuit, Paris said she put her possessions in storage two years ago when she and her sister, Nicky, moved out of a house that had been broken into by burglars. Paris insisted that a removal company was supposed to pay the storage fees and was 'shocked and surprised' to know that her belongings were sold at public auction. The lawsuit claimed that defendants Nabil and Nabila Haniss paid $2,775 for the contents of the storage unit and later sold the items for $10 million to entrepreneur Bardia Persa, who created the parisexposed.com site.

'Monthly invoices were sent to her accountant, and they were paid up,' said Mintz. 'Paris is very angry. She's been victimized. These are private diaries and memories. It's an awful thing.'

'I was appalled to learn that people are exploiting me

and my sisters' private personal belongings for commercial gain,' said a still-shocked Paris. She added that the Website was 'one of the single most egregious and reprehensible invasions of privacy ever committed against an individual.' A federal judge quickly issued a temporary injunction against the site, a move welcomed by Mintz who raged, 'I know what this has done personally and emotionally to Paris. As far as I'm concerned, this is the most disturbing intrusion upon the privacy of a public figure that I've ever witnessed.' Although the injunction closed down the site, this episode was another reminder of the realities of fame.

Given the nature of the headlines that surrounded the parisexposed.com stories, Paris was relieved by the step taken by the Associated Press news agency, which banned its journalists from filing stories about her for a week. We just wanted to see what would happen,' said an editor. The agency's entertainment editor, Jesse Washington, announced the ban to staff through an official memo. 'There was a surprising amount of hand wringing. A lot of people in the newsroom were saying this was tampering with the news.' In reality, it seemed to be more of a publicity stunt designed to attract attention to the agency – and a typically hypocritical move from a Paris-basher.

Next up came Paris's 26th birthday party at the Prime Grill restaurant in Beverly Hills, which was ruined when a man started upsetting other guests by paying particular attention to American Idol judge Paula Abdul. 'He was hurling flowers and pieces of foam at her,' a source said.

'He then started speaking gibberish in an Arabic accent, mocking her Syrian ancestry.' Abdul was planning to sing *Happy Birthday* to Paris but was so offended that she walked out.

The offending guest then started haranguing Courtney Love and her 14-year-old daughter. 'He lifted her up so she was straddling his waist,' said a partygoer. 'Her dress was riding up as he made lewd suggestions and simulated sex in front of her daughter.' Still not satisfied, he then made a lunge for the expensive necklace Paris was wearing. Paris started crying and the man was asked to leave.

The controversy was just beginning, though. Shortly after the party, Love posted the following on her Website: 'I went into the bathroom and there was a mountain of — gee, well — it was powder and it was white. Wonder if it was sugar?' Paris strongly denies having anything to do with illegal drugs. She says, 'I've seen girls out now who've been doing it for so long they look haggard and old. I like my young face. I don't want to look old.'

Whatever the truth of Love's allegation, it had clearly been quite a night. The *Daily Mirror*'s 3am Girls attended and reported that all guests were handed silver pens on arrival and told to write birthday messages on a huge poster of Paris. On entering the main room, they were confronted by 'a full-size lap-dancing pole and an enormous portrait of publicity-shy Paris herself ... The dining room boasted a chandeliers and yet another gargantuan image of the heiress.' The girls concluded: 'Paris, can't wait for your 27th!'

If the early months of 2007 were tough for Paris, they were also tricky for Britney Spears. The young pop star was full of praise for how much Paris had helped her in the aftermath of her split from Kevin Federline. Paris dressed herself and Spears in matching blue tutus and they danced the night away at her house. Spears said, 'She told me I had wasted years looking after that scumbag and the only way I can get over him once and for all is to let my hair down with my friends and go wild for a while. She was so right, I'm having such a great time.' However, both Spears and Paris were soon getting stick galore from the media, with many suggesting that Spears was behaving in an inappropriate way given that she is a mother.

It seemed that Paris had decided to defend her new best friend when the following MySpace bulletin was attributed to her: 'I told Brit I'd write a bulletin on here to try to clear some news to at least the people who are on my list. Lately, you've been seeing pics of me and Britney partying (blah blah) and she knows that some of her fans are very upset about what they call her "behaviour" and sadly they're blaming the issue on her being friends with me. Yeah, me and Brit have become really close in the past few weeks, and we've gone out a lot in the past few nights, but I never influence anything she does, and neither does anyone else.

'Brit is her own person and she deals with her own things everyday. For people to call out her parenting skills on behalf of her partying ethics is appalling. Britney loves her kids to death and I know for a fact that it truly hurts her when she sees these cruel things being written about her. She goes home every night to her babies and partying has not come in the way of her parenting.

'Anyone who has called her out on this should really be ashamed. There are thousands of mothers out there who like to go out and have a good time. But, you do not see people out there calling them 'bad parents' She's young, and if she wants to go out and have some fun, let her. Just because she does these things does not mean she doesn't care about her children. For the sake of Britney and her kids, be kind. Love, Paris.'

However, Mintz denied that Paris had written this bulletin. 'Did she write that piece?' he said, 'No, she did not. I have no idea who did. There are dozens and dozens of people that use the Web, that write things and post pictures and identify themselves as Paris. There are at least 80 of them. The Web is a bit like the Wild West – somewhat uncontrollable.'

Whoever wrote it, there was no doubt that Spears was soon trying to distance herself from Paris. Britney's spokesperson told reporters: 'Britney had fun with Paris. But she wants to focus on her family and career now.' Not that this was the final word on the matter. Paris had been invited to the Opera Ball in Vienna by Richard Lugner. Wealthy entrepreneur Lugner had previously invited Geri Halliwell, Pamela Anderson and Carmen Electra to the lavish evening where boxes cost up to £15,000. He also invited Spears to the event but following her falling out with Paris, the pop star's invitation was withdrawn. 'Paris will no longer be joined by Britney,' said Lugner's wife Christina. 'They unfortunately do not get on any more. But Paris is very happy.' Sources close to Spears described her as a 'secret opera fan' and said she was furious to be 'uninvited'. They added that the feud was not over.

In any case, the trip did not prove to be quite as enjoyable as Paris hoped. As soon as the Austrian media heard of her impending arrival, they kept a special eye on the headlines relating to her, including those surrounding the contents of parisexposed.com, and others suggesting that alongside porn legend Jenna Jameson she was due to appear on a reality television show teaching male virgins how to have sex. Sure enough, the media found some sour faces to say that Paris should not be allowed to attend. 'This makes a farce of the Opera Ball,' said Barbara Kroth, a retired real-estate agent who says she is a regular at the event 'because of the quality it represents.' However, Mr Lugner was quick to defend Paris. 'Look, there are probably three or four nude photos of me, too, stashed away somewhere,' he shrugged. Support was also forthcoming from Elisabeth Guertler, who oversees the evening. 'I've never asked any other guests what they do in their private lives,' she said.

So the trip went ahead for Paris but the journey hit a snag when she discovered en route to Vienna that her passport had expired. But Susan McCaw, the US ambassador to Austria, saved the day and ensured that the blushing heiress was still allowed entry to the country.

Soon after her arrival, Paris had a scheduled appearance

at a shopping mall to make. 'Hello everybody, it's so good to see you,' she said to the crowd. 'Happy late Valentine's Day!' A cheer went up but then Paris was suddenly pelted with objects thrown by some of the crowd. The objects included cigarette packs, tissues and lipsticks. The Austrian Press Agency reported that the chaos was planned by a communist youth organization. Paris said that being pelted was 'no big deal' and she still loved her fans. Finally, two days later came the Opera Ball itself, which was covered live on television in Austria. Some of the footage of her in the audience was interpreted by the broadcasters to suggest that Paris was bored. 'Look how excited she is,' said a sarcastic commentator for public television station ORF.

So much for opera, what about pop? Paris was keen to look ahead in her music career as proved when she contacted Robbie Williams to see if he would be willing to hook up with her musically. She sent him a solid gold fountain pen worth £2,500 and a note which read: 'I know you like angels and if you want one to come into your life just write me into it with a song, a beautiful shining song.'

It emerged that through her friendship with Victoria Beckham – 'She's my favourite Wag! She's gorgeous. I always wear her jeans. They're hot!' – she had had dinner with Simon Cowell, who offered her some advice on her pop career. 'He said he likes my music,' confirmed Paris.

Not everyone was excited at the thought of Williams recording with Paris. Vanessa Feltz wrote: 'Get ready for the Clash of the Egos. If Robbie Williams and Paris Hilton really do get it on, skyscrapers will crumble, governments will fall and Wall Street will very probably crash. The two are monumental show-offs, hopelessly addicted to attention and used to the entire known universe bowing, scraping and falling at their feet. The power struggle in their relationship would be compulsive viewing. Watch as they compete for most neurotic, most sexually predatory and most vulnerable.'

Good news followed, though, when in April it was revealed that 607,375 copies of her debut album *Paris* had been sold worldwide and that the album had therefore been certified Gold in the United States.

Some reports have suggested that Paris has given up on music as a career. However, she seems to be as keen on it as ever and claims that one of the world's leading pop idols is keen to link up with her. Justin Timberlake has sold over 13 millions albums worldwide and has worked with Snoop Dogg, Nelly and super-cool producers The Neptunes and Timbaland. Now, it seems he wants to work with Paris. 'I think we blend well and he says he has something in mind for both of us,' she smiled. 'I can't wait.'

Paris was also linked with another male pop star around this time – but in a different way. She was spotted dancing with James Blunt at Los Angeles nightclub Teddy's. 'Paris and James danced and held hands. Then they started to make out.' Another eye witness said, 'They were all over each other. Paris was hanging on his every word and they ended up at her house.' There, they were joined by her sister and Nicky's boyfriend, David Katzenberg. A few days later she was seen partying with rapper Kevin Federline, Britney Spears' ex-boyfriend.

An artist who is extremely unlikely to ever hook-up musically or romantically with Paris is brattish British pop star Lily Allen, who let rip at Paris when a music channel banned her single. 'I got really offended when my single *Smile* got banned [during after-school hours] from MTV in the UK, because it had the word f*ck in it,' she moaned. 'They said, "We don't want kids to grow up too quickly." But then you have Paris Hilton and the Pussycat Dolls taking their clothes off and gyrating up against womanizing, asshole men, and that's acceptable. You're thinking your kids are gonna grow up quicker because they heard the word f*ck than from thinking they should be shoving their tits in people's faces?'

One of the men that Paris was been linked to in 2007 was both a musician and actor, who has been compared to Justin Timberlake. Born in Dallas, Texas on 25 October 1981, Josh Henderson spent most of his formative years in Oklahoma and Texas in America's south and studied at Tulsa Memorial High School. He competed in the second series of reality television show *Popstars*, where he stood out and was noted for 'singing like Justin Timberlake'. He made it through to the final and was one of six winners who formed the band Scene 23. Although the band never released a record, Henderson says he learned lots from his experience. 'I was thrown into the business,' he says. 'It was kind of a crash course. I had to soak everything up because I gave up my life for that show.'

He moved on to acting and appeared in several seasons of the sitcom *One On One* and then moved to the hit ABC show *8 Simple Rules... for Dating my Teenage Daughter*. There, he met Kaley Cuoco who became his girlfriend for a while. After breaking up with her he appeared on *The Ashlee Simpson Show* and began to date the leading lady. The couple were together for two years. After he and Simpson broke up, Henderson said, 'We are still very close. People go through a lot together, and I'm all for helping her out. She's really talented, and I'm very happy for her.'

Henderson and Paris met on Friday night at Les Deux and ended up kissing on the couch like two giddy teenagers. 'It was really cute,' a witness said. Paris and Josh then sat in the backseat of the car by themselves for about 15 minutes. 'It was just the two of them talking and flirting. I guess they wanted to have some alone time before heading to Paris's house where she had a St. Patrick's Day party.' Elliot Mintz was approached about the reports linking Paris with Henderson and said, 'Matters of that nature are only the business of the two people involved. Josh treats Paris with great respect and dignity. He is not a "Hollywood guy". Paris seems very comfortable around him.' So were they friends or more than friends? Another source maintained that Paris wasn't interested in a relationship with Henderson or any other man 'She's into just hanging out with her girlfriends.'

Henderson has one blue eye and one green eye, a condition known as heterochromia, but around this time, Paris decided to literally turn her brown eyes blue when she invested in some tinted contacts. However, shortly after this she had to visit a plastic surgeon's office to 'fix her drooping left eyelid', a source claimed. Paris secretly had surgery in 2001 to lift her lids. The muscles of her left eye were supposedly damaged as a result, 'causing it to droop more than the right one'. Paris made the problem worse by wearing blue-tinted contact lenses over her brown irises and ignoring doctors' orders to stop wearing tinted lenses, according to the *New York Post*.

So much for work on her eyes, had Paris also had some work done a little lower down her body? The question that buzzed around Paris throughout the first half of 2007 was 'Has she had a boob job?' Such speculation was not entirely new to Paris, though. Back in 2004, a source close to her said, 'A year ago Paris was telling friends she'd never get breast implants. She loves being natural but now she seems to be caving in to peer pressure. Everywhere she looks she sees cleavage. So it's not a surprise that she is considering it. But Paris is a babe already and sometimes big doesn't mean better.'

A year later, she appeared on a German television show looking particularly busty. During the filming she was constantly checking her cleavage, which only served to fuel the speculation. Then, in 2006, she was spotted visiting a Los Angeles plastic surgery clinic. A magazine had recently speculated that she might be pregnant and reportedly furious at this conclusion being drawn from her appearance, Paris visited the clinic seeking advice about a tummy tuck.

With all this speculation surrounding her, Paris ruled out having a boob job and said he was thrilled to be on the flat side. 'When I was 13, I really wanted a boob job because all my friends started to have boobs. But you know what? I like being flat. I think it's hot. I never have to wear a bra.' However, in February 2007 a series of paparazzi photographs that showed Paris looking very busty sent speculation about her chest into overdrive. 'Where did they come from Paris?' ran the headline in the *Star*. The accompanying story read: 'It looks like Paris Hilton has suddenly become an even bigger celebrity than before. Well, it was certainly a case of Hollywood AND bust for the 25-year-old heiress as she headed for LA hangout the Hyde Club. She filled her low-cut dress like never before – prompting onlookers to wonder if the previously flat-chested blonde had supersized herself.'

At the *Sun*, the speculation continued. 'Paris or Bust!' echoed the tabloid newspaper. 'The 25-year-old had no room to spare in her low-cut baby doll dress on a nightie out in Hollywood. Celebrity-watchers were left guessing whether she'd got her top-floor lift from a plastic surgeon – or was just wearing a powerful push-up bra. Her breasts seemed massive. Everyone was staring. She's known for her quite small boobs, so it's a surprise to see her busting out of her top.'

One newspaper enlisted the help of plastic surgeon to

the stars Alex Karidis. He told them, 'It looks like Paris has put on a bit of weight so her breasts might be fuller. And she could have got a push-up bra. But Paris didn't have much to fill a bra before and there's a lot more fullness to the top of the breast. You wouldn't expect her to naturally have those size breasts.'

Hot on the heels of this, she was snapped leaving Brett Ratner's Hollywood birthday party and seemed to be positively spilling out of her top. An onlooker said, 'Paris looked sensational in a tight top and tiny shorts. Nobody could take their eyes off her boobs. They looked very full and there was plenty of cleavage. Lots of people were taking pictures of them on their mobiles.' The American press was just as fascinated. The Arizona Republic, amusingly, reported on 'the mystery of Paris Hilton's ballooning bazooms'. One night she got so fed up with the girls talking about her in the ladies room of an LA club that she pulled open her top and showed everyone present that she was hiding nothing but a very expensive bra.

One chain of nightclubs that Paris is unlikely to ever darken the door of again are any of the ones that she had previously endorsed, Club Paris. Club owner Fred Khalilian revealed that Paris's endorsement deal with the clubs was over because she had failed to turn up for scheduled appearances in Orlando, and because the relenting media glare on Paris had got so huge that he was no longer in his comfort zone. 'She's created a circus for herself,' he said. 'It's all about: How has she screwed up now? I was basically sick of hearing "Where is Paris? Where is Paris?"

The troubles started two years ago when Hilton showed up six hours late for the grand opening of the first club. 'I was in the Swiss Alps skiing, and I got caught at the airport with all the holiday travel so I've been trying to travel for the past 24 hours. I'm so sorry I'm late,' Paris said at the time. Khalilian denied that losing Paris's endorsement would cause the club any problems. 'I personally think the club is going to do better. She didn't exist anyway.' Elliot Mintz described Khalilian's comments as 'unfortunate'.

However, even after she'd been fired, Paris's name continued to adorn the club, which announced via its Website a novel way of recruiting a new face to endorse the chain. 'Club Paris presents The Replacement Miss Club Paris USA coming soon,' read the homepage. 'Audition dates, times and network to be announced'. So this was going to be a reality television style affair? Yes, said Khalilian. 'It's going to happen like *American Idol* or *Making The Band*. It will be a nationwide thing.'

As her relationship with the club chain came to a disappointing end, Paris's relationship with Nicole Richie was rekindled. Paris says it was a simple rebirth. 'It was Nicole's birthday and I really missed her, and I just decided to pick up the phone and call her.' The pair both agree that once they hooked up again, it was as if they had never been apart. Richie said, 'We just got together that night and it was like there was never anything that happened. It was weird, like we had seen each other yesterday.' Paris is keen to put their differences firmly in the past and she strongly disputes some of the media coverage that has been afforded to their row. 'Everyone has a fight, you know. It's just not going to be publicised, you know, and have things construed and changed around. You know, we're friends. We know the truth. The media made up a lot of silly stories and you just have to not pay attention to it.'

With their differences patched up, Paris and Richie were ready to start filming the fifth season of *The Simple Life*. As the fourth season had shown, the whole thing rather fell down when Paris and Richie were no longer friends. Paris agrees that the true appeal of the show is not about rich girls slumming it, but about friendship. 'It works because it's about two best friends who are together and I think people can relate to that, because everyone has a best friend,' she smiles. 'We have our secret languages and our secret looks to each other and we just have fun together. I don't know. It's hard to find a group who can be like that together.'

The original title for the season was *Malibu: Camp Simple Life*, but this was later replaced with *The Simple Life Goes to Camp*. The show sees the pair working as counsellors at Camp Shawnee in the mountains near Los Angeles. This, the programme-makers felt, saw the show go back to basics. 'The fact that Paris and Nicole are friends again and will have to survive without their luxuries at a family-run camp in the middle of nowhere takes us back full circle to the original concept that makes this show so much fun,' says Lisa Berger, of E! Networks. 'For this season, we are putting the girls into completely unfamiliar situations, sitting back and watching them in action, which is what made this show a hit right out of the gate.'

During the filming of the show, Richie attracted a lot of concern for her increasingly skinny physique. 'Four or five times she's felt really faint and almost passed out,' a source said. 'She has to go into her trailer for a good part of the day.' She was diagnosed with hypoglycaemia. However, the filming went well and the show was set to be a big hit. Paris says she learned a great deal from her five seasons of *The Simple Life* but the biggest lesson she took from the experience concerned her friendship with Richie. 'I've learned that we can survive any situation and we can have fun no matter where we are as long as we're together,' she grinned.

Paris took some time out from filming to launch her signature DreamCatchers European hair extensions at the annual Chicago Midwest Beauty Show in Rosemont. Clad in jeans, red patent leather heels and a jewel-encrusted black top, she happily struck poses and signed autographs. 'Hair is such an important part of my everyday life,' she said. 'I wear a different hairstyle everyday, and I want great hair to be easy for everyone.' After wearing the extensions for the past few months, Paris decided to tie her name to the product. 'It's something I really believe in,' she cooed. 'I want my fans to feel great, to feel sexy.' Fans Mary Meneghin and Joanna Gierczyk were overjoyed to meet Paris in the flesh at the launch. 'This is worth the trip!' Meneghin said. On her way back to the set of *The Simple Life*, Paris shopped at the Field Museum store at Chicago's O'Hare International Airport for a spot of shopping. She spent £125 on soft toys and then casually hopped on to an electric cart that whisked away to her flight back to LA.

Another new endorsement for Paris came in the form of a clothing line with the BBC Apparel Group. No relation to the broadcasting company, BBC is a multi-million pound US clothing firm. It has obtained the master license for Paris Inc., which gives them full control of the brand. It started with sportswear but further additions seem highly likely in the near future. Paris was very much a hands-on celebrity endorser, in keeping with her workaholic tendencies. 'She has also been and will continue to be very involved with the brand,' said Deke Jamieson, senior vice president of marketing and licensing at Dollhouse, a division of BBC Apparel Group. 'She comes in, meets with designers, works with them here in New York and in California. She has made a commitment to this and is serious about it. Many celebrities just lend their names to a label. That's not enough. Paris wants to wear the product and play an integral role in designing the product. This is not just a logo slap. This is a huge brand undertaking for us and we are very ready for it.'

Animal-lover Paris spent Easter 2007 with two real black and white bunnies. Wearing a Farrah Fawcett-style brunette wig and sailing-themed cardie and top, she went shopping in the Beverly Centre to hunt for rabbits. 'Paris has lots of little dogs and a ferret, she fancied a different animal to play with for a change so she went out and bought two bunnies.'

Paris's love of animals shows no sign of abating but how strong is the media's love affair with her? Under the headline 'Who's got IT down to a tee?' The *Sun* newspaper pitched the Hilton sisters against Pixie and Peaches, the Geldof sisters, in the ultimate battle of the It-girl siblings. The report began, 'The Geldofs, Peaches and Pixie, are fast becoming the UK equivalent of those notorious Hilton sisters. Both sets of siblings have a wealthy dad, they kick up a storm on the social scene, they like to rock the latest styles from the fashion pages and they know how to knock back an almighty tipple or three. So which of these stylish sets of socialites can boast the crown of World's Leading It Girls?' Over six rounds, the Hiltons won.

As Paris continued to branch out her various business and artistic ventures, what could stop her?

16

COURT IN THE ACT

The Los Angeles Superior Court is an austere building with an austere air about it. However, when Paris Hilton was due to appear there with the threat of prison hanging over her head, it took on the sort of heady, manic atmosphere that she is used to facing at film premieres and other exclusive social events. Photographers lined up at the entrance and were taped off into press sections. One onlooker was short and sweet when asked to describe the scene: 'It was a zoo out there today'. It was almost like a scene from a great American novel: the rich socialite being thrown to the wolves of the media and legal system. The scent of blood was in the air. Tom Wolfe would have killed for such a yarn.

The media frenzy had been building for months; the newspapers and television had tried to portray Paris as being out of control just as they had when she and Nicole partied as teenagers in Manhattan. This time, though, the media were unequivocal: Paris, they said, was headed for disaster. 'She might be smiling on the outside but deep down she is really unhappy right now,' said an unnamed 'friend' of Paris. 'She knows she'll lose a lot of work if she gets a reputation as someone who has done time. Her whole career is based on her image and maintaining a fan base – she has nothing else to rely on. She's petrified.

'People in the industry are taking her less seriously than before and she doesn't feel like she's Hollywood's golden girl anymore. She's the butt of quite a few jokes in LA these days and she hates it. She's been crying a lot, especially when she's been drinking and is scared that her life is falling apart.'

Whatever the truth of those quotes, there certainly was a storm gathering over her head. Under the headline Dead Naked Paris On Display, a report in the *Sun*'s Bizarre page began: 'I thought nothing could shock me when it came to Paris Hilton – but an American artist has managed it.' Artist Daniel Edwards had recently unveiled a piece called *The Paris Hilton Autopsy*. The life-size clay sculpture of Paris's corpse featured her wearing a tiara, with Tinkerbell at her side and a BlackBerry in her hand. The corpse was displayed at Capla Kesting Fine Art gallery in Brooklyn, surrounded by information and literature about drunken driving. Gallery director David Kesting says the piece counters 'the disturbingly glamorized trend of Hollywood's "girls gone wild".' This was like Banksy's album protest all over again but it did reflect fears of where Paris was headed to.

The threat of jail hanging over Paris was very real. As part of her probation for the drink driving charge, her driving privileges were suspended from November 30 to March 31. A letter reiterating the suspension was sent to her Beverly Hills business office. However, officers caught her driving three times during the ban. In December she was stopped in Hollywood by a police officer for making an illegal turn and warned that her licence was not valid. Then on January 15, a California Highway Patrol officer stopped Hilton in Culver City for having no licence plates on the front or back of her car. The officer also informed her that she was driving on a suspended licence and – crucially – she signed a document acknowledging that she was not allowed to drive.

Then, on February 27, she was pulled over for speeding on Sunset Boulevard with her headlights off – she was still suspended from driving at this point, yet there she was – driving her blue 2007 Bentley Continental GTC Convertible. 'Officers became suspicious when they saw a car speeding along Sunset Boulevard with no headlights on,' said a spokesman from LA Sheriff's Headquarters Bureau. She was arrested for driving on a suspended licence, which is a misdemeanour. Her car was impounded and she was cited and released.' Paris was returning home from buying some DVDs at Virgin Megastore in West Hollywood after spending the day at home for a photo shoot, Elliot Mintz said. He insisted that his client didn't realise the headlights were not on because she had just left a brightly-lit car park.

This was the final straw for the city prosecutors. 'Our office is waiting to obtain a copy of the citation,' said Nick Velasquez, a spokesman for the Los Angeles city attorney's office. 'Once we're able to verify that Miss Hilton was driving the vehicle, we will request that the court revoke her probation and set a probation violation hearing.' He added that jail was a possibility for Paris. However, Paris told *Harpers* magazine that she felt the police stop her only because of her fame. 'The cops do it all the time. They'll just pull me over to hit on me. It's really annoying. They're like, "What's your phone number? Want to go to dinner?"'

However, this was not going to be enough to mount a defence in court and ominously, the week before the hearing, the Kansas City Star reported: 'Just Thursday, the California legislature approved $7.4 billion for more prison beds. Maybe they know something we don't.'

What was known was that the city prosecutor had vowed that he would be asking the judge to sentence her to 45 days in prison for violating the terms of probation that she had been handed at her hearing for drink driving. She had been said to be nervous of the hearing; one friend claims Paris told her: 'My life will be over if I spend any time, even just one day, in jail'. However, arriving 10 minutes late for the hearing did not give her a good start. Wearing a grey jacket, white blouse, black trousers, Christian Louboutin heels, and carrying a Chanel bag, Hilton swung her hips as she entered the court via a side entrance.

COURT IN THE ACT

The courtroom itself took on a surreal air too. The press bench was more packed than ever and nine bailiffs were present, more than would be used for even a high-profile murder case. As she entered the courtroom, Paris looked impassive as she mingled with her parents for a while. Both were wearing black suits. Kathy carried a beige Hermes bag. When Paris sat between her lawyers, she pulled a compact mirror from her black clutch purse and checked her make-up. Then the courtroom turned electrifyingly silent as Paris took to the witness stand for 30 minutes. One journalist present gave her praise for her performance and described her as 'a good witness.' Paris testified that she was under the false impression that her licence had been suspended for just 30 days following the September arrest and that she would be allowed to drive for work purposes for three months after that. She blamed the misunderstanding on Elliot Mintz, who also took to the witness stand and backed up what she said.

Paris told the judge: 'I followed the laws. I was told my licence was suspended for 30 days. If it wasn't work-related, it'd be my assistant driving me or we would call a car service. I wanted to follow the rules.' She added: 'I did what I was told. I followed the law and I respect the law,' she told Judge Michael T. Sauer. 'I want you to know I'm very sorry. It makes me upset and angry. I was given wrong information. I want to say I'm sorry.' Asked about the paper she had signed following the January traffic stop, she said she did not read what she was signing. 'I was just signing it because the officer told me to,' she said.

This led to some jokes and banter between the judge and the defence attorneys. Rick and Kathy were visibly angry at these light-hearted exchanges.

Just before the sentence was announced, Paris was invited to make one last statement to the court. She stood up and spoke to the judge from the heart. 'I'm very sorry, and from now on I'm going to pay complete attention to everything. I'm sorry, and I did not do it on purpose at all,' she told the judge. She got visibly choked up as she said these words.

However, the judge completely dismissed Paris and Mintz's protestations. 'I can't believe that either attorney did not tell her that the suspension had been upheld,' he said. 'She wanted to disregard everything that was said and continue to drive no matter what.' He ruled that she was in violation of the terms of her probation and told her she would have to serve 45 days in prison. Paris gasped and then broke down in tears. 'I don't understand. I did what they told me,' she sobbed and laid her head down on the defendant's table as the courtroom erupted in pandemonium.

Kathy had kept up a running commentary throughout the hearing, making sneering comments during the city prosecutor's statements such as 'Yeah, right,' and 'this is just a pathetic reality show' and 'You're pathetic!' She had also rolled her eyes and sighed at regular intervals throughout the prosecutor's words. However, when sentencing was passed, she screamed at the judge 'May I have your autograph?!' – to imply that the judge was attempting to gain celebrity by sentencing her daughter to jail. The judge responded by slamming down his gavel and shouting the immortal words: 'Order in the court!'

Paris's parents rushed forward to try and console her but were blocked by a sheriff's deputy. Kathy snapped: 'Don't touch me! You touched my breast!' Eventually, Paris was led out of court with a police escort, and was heard to snap: 'They're doing this because it's me.' Outside the court, her lawyer Howard Weitzman was equally dismissive. 'I've been in this business many, many, many years and I am shocked and disappointed by the sentence imposed by the judge,' said the much-respected Weitzman, who has previously represented OJ Simpson. 'To sentence Paris Hilton to jail for 45 days – to me – was uncalled for, inappropriate and bordered on the ludicrous.' He added: 'I think she was singled out because she is who she is. I've been involved in cases and know of cases where people have second and third driving-under-the-influence convictions and don't go to jail.' Weitzman said he would appeal 'to modify the sentence'. However, city attorney spokesman Nick Velasquez said that the judge's ruling 'sends a clear message that in the city of Los Angeles, no one is above the law. She violated the law and appropriate action was taken.' Jeffrey Isaacs, chief of the Criminal Branch of the LA City Attorney's office said that Paris's fate could have been even worse: 'This was well within the judge's discretion and more than just, she could've got 90 days.'

As the Hilton entourage left the court, her parents

were asked one final time what they thought of the sentence, allowing Kathy one more angry outburst. 'This is pathetic and disgusting, a waste of taxpayer money with all this nonsense,' she slammed before the family piled into their black people carrier and were driven off.

Meanwhile, the judge wanted Paris to go straight to jail but her attorneys argued for a delay, stating that she had lots of personal matters that needed to be attended to before going away. Judge Sauer agreed, but ruled that she would not be allowed any work release outings, use of an alternative jail or electronic monitoring instead of jail. He also ruled out the option of Paris paying to serve time in a jail of her choice, an option that is permitted in Californian law.

The media went into overdrive as the news broke, with Fox News covering the story more or less non-stop all evening. Within hours of the hearing, thousands of T-shirts were rushed to shops bearing slogans like 'Liberate Paris'. Support was also forthcoming from Paris's friend Mario Lavandeira. 'I think she will emerge [from jail] with a certain respect and dignity,' he said. 'Like Snoop Dogg.'

'It will actually increase her star appeal,' agreed star publicist Michael Levine. 'There's a segment of our society that's somehow engaged in the soap opera that is Paris Hilton, and this a very compelling plot line in the soap opera.' A source close to Lindsay Lohan said: 'Lindsay feels bad for her and is sympathetic to anyone going through a hard time.'

The jail chosen by the judge for Paris to go through a

hard time at was the Century Regional Detention Facility in Lynwood, California. With more than 2,100 inmates, the Facility is Los Angeles's only jail for women. It has previously held actresses Darryl Hannah and *Lost* star Michelle Rodriguez, though only for a matter of hours and days respectively. Inmates there are permitted to leave their cells for only an hour each day to shower, watch television, participate in outdoor recreation or talk on the telephone. There is a bank of payphones – mobile phones and Blackberry handsets are not allowed. Prisoners are fed three low-sodium meals a day. Beef and pork are never on the menu – poultry is the only meat served. Paris's cell was to be 12-by-8 feet with a toilet, sink and a window 6 inches wide.

Quite a step-down for anyone, but a massive one for Paris, who grew up in the Waldorf-Astoria. As the *Guardian* report the day following the sentencing put it: 'The average Hilton hotel room offers a comfy bed and en suite bathroom. The average room in the women's jail in Lynwood, south Los Angeles, offers a lumpy cot and an en suite, open plan toilet.' However, Paris was lucky to avoid the horrific Twin Towers County Jail which is home to California's most brutal inmates. As the Sheriff's Department said: 'She's an obvious target and it will be far easier to keep her safe in Lynwood.' A former inmate of the Twin Towers said: 'Paris should count herself very lucky she escaped Twin Towers. She'd have needed a personal guard 24/7 there. But Lynwood could be dangerous for her too – even if she's in a segregation block. It can be brutal and debilitating – and they'd better keep a very close eye on Paris because there are a few lesbian "mamas" in there who would just love to get their claws on her.' Defence attorney Sean Tabibian dismissed these fears: 'Her biggest problem is going to be boredom,' said the attorney, who has many clients at the jail. 'How many conversations can you have with yourself?'

When she got home after the sentencing, Paris stayed up all night. 'She doesn't want to eat,' a source said. Her on-off boyfriend Stavros Niarchos was on-hand to offer his commiseration. 'She goes from crying to being furious,' said the source. 'Paris is petrified and that's putting it mildly. She is not a normal citizen and fears very strongly she'll be attacked by someone wanting to make a name for themselves.'

Her first public appearance following the sentencing came the following day when she went shopping with her mother at Francis-Orr and Ermenegildo in Beverly Hills before grabbing lunch at Prego. She broke down during the meal and held her head in her hands. 'I told the truth yesterday,' she told photographers. 'I feel that I was treated unfairly and that the sentence is both cruel and unwanted and I don't deserve this.' Her parents were meanwhile busy trying to work out how to get her sentence reduced. They reportedly approached politicians, including California governor Arnold Schwarzenegger. The governor was already being lobbied by Paris's army of fans, one of whom opened an online petition to Schwarzenegger on Paris's MySpace page. 'She provides hope for young people all over the US and the world,' opened the petition. 'She provides beauty and excitement to (most of) our otherwise mundane lives.' Paris was quick to thank the fan. 'I just want to thank Joshua so much for his kind words of love and support. God Bless. Love Paris.'

Meanwhile, a zany protest group known as The Resistance announced that they planned to mount a public demonstration against Paris by binning copies of her CD outside the Beverly Hills Hilton on the day Paris started her sentence. 'The kinds of role models that have come to light recently in America are horrible role models,' founder Mark Dice said. 'We're going to be throwing her CDs in huge trash cans and getting them off the face of the Earth,' he added.

As she waited for the sentence to start, Paris turned to a higher power for support. First, she was spotted shopping at the Buddhist store Bodhi Tree in Hollywood. Then she was seen carrying a Bible. She was often photographed wearing white during this period, with reporters speculating that this was in an attempt to appear pure. To the same end, she also reduced her partying to an absolute minimum. Paris' lawyers ordered her to, in effect, live like a nun. 'They have ordered her to show a judge she has some humility and social responsibility if she is going to have her sentence reduced on appeal,' said a friend. 'That means no booze, no parading round in skimpy outfits, no partying. She's got to stick with her family and take on a healthier regime.'

Some respite was offered to Paris when the Los Angeles County sheriff's office announced that she could end up serving less than the 45 days. 'Hilton, sentenced last week to do the time, could spend three weeks or less behind bars because of a state requirement that grants inmates time off for good behaviour and because of overcrowding in the system,' said a spokesman. When it was confirmed that Paris's sentence would be cut to 23 days, she told her lawyer to drop their planned appeal and announced that she would grit her teeth and serve the 23 days. To help her get through the sentence, Paris announced that she planned to keep a diary of her prison experiences and hoped to sell the contents on release.

As the clock ticked down to the deadline by which she had to report to jail, Paris attended the MTV Awards wearing a stunning black strapless dress with glittering jewels. She posed for photographers and then spoke to the reporters who naturally wanted to know how she felt about her impending imprisonment. 'I am trying to be strong right now,' she said. 'I've received thousands of letters from around the world of support and it's really been inspirational and really helped me. I'm really scared but I'm ready to do this. And I hope that I'm an example to other young people.'

Once inside the theatre for the ceremony, Paris was the target of jokes from comedienne Sarah Silverman. 'In a couple of days, Paris Hilton is going to jail,' said Silverman. 'The judge says that it's going to be a no-frills thing and that is ridiculous. She is totally going to get special treatment. As a matter of fact, I heard that to make her feel more comfortable in prison, the guards are going to paint the bars to look like penises. I think it's wrong, too. I just worry that she's going to break her teeth on those things.'

Paris could afford to keep these jokes in perspective because she was the only person in the venue who knew she was going to report to jail within hours of the ceremony finishing. So it was that at 11.38 p.m. on Sunday June 3, 2007, Paris Whitney Hilton became prisoner number 9818783. She surrendered her possessions, was strip-searched and photographed. She was also issued jail clothing, an orange top and pants and personal hygiene items. 'She was cooperative during the process, which included being fingerprinted, photographed and medically screened,' a Sheriff's Department statement said. Then at 1 a.m. she was led to her cell which she had all to herself and which was segregated from the main prison population. Her first meal behind bars was cereal, bread and fruit juice.

'I am ready to face the consequences of violating probation,' she said in a statement released by her lawyer that evening. 'During the past few weeks I have had a lot of time to think and have come to realize I made some mistakes. This is an important point in my life and I need to take responsibility for my actions. In the future, I plan on taking more of an active role in the decisions I make. I want to thank my family, friends and fans for their continued support. Although I am scared, I am ready to begin my jail sentence.' However, anyone who thought that she was going to just quietly do her time had a rude awakening in almost immediate store.

On her second day in jail, the lady who trademarked the catchphrase 'that's hot' complained that her cell was too cold. She also moaned that because she had no pillow, she was being forced to bunch up blankets to improvise one. Paris said she was losing her appetite and complained about the noise being made by other prisoners. Not that her fellow inmates were meaning to intimidate her. Their new celebrity inmate was popular and chants of 'Paris! Paris! Paris!' were heard. One made an origami butterfly as a gift for Paris and slipped it under her cell door. Another gave her a drawing book to help pass the 23 hours she was spending alone in her cell.

All the same, life in prison was taking a heavy toll on Paris. 'She cries all day,' said a prison source. 'She looks unwashed, she has no makeup and her hair is tangled. She cried audibly through the first two nights.' Just three days into Paris's sentence, the world was stunned as news broke that she was being released on orders of the county sheriff because of an unspecified medical condition and that she'd serve the remainder of her sentence under house arrest at her mansion. 'I can't specifically talk about the medical situation other than to say that, yes, it played a part in this,' said the sheriff's spokesman.

Through her lawyer, Paris expressed her relief at this development. 'I want to thank the Los Angeles County Sheriff's Department and staff of the Century Regional

Detention Center for treating me fairly and professionally. I am going to serve the remaining 40 days of my sentence [at home]. I have learned a great deal from this ordeal and hope that others have learned from my mistakes.'

Her relief was short-lived, though. Within hours of her release, Judge Michael T. Sauer, who had originally sentenced her, demanded that she return to court the following day. When he had sentenced Hilton to jail, the judge had ruled specifically that she could not serve her sentence at home under electronic monitoring. The following day, a shaken Paris was driven to court in a sheriff's car. She had embraced family members before getting into the car. Her mother told her: 'It is what it is and it's in God's hands now. It's out of our hands. There's nothing we can do.'

After being photographed crying in the back seat of the car, Paris appeared to be in a terrible state in court. Onlookers described her as looking to be in immense mental and physical pain. Her torment went to new levels when the judge ordered her to return to jail and serve the remainder of the 45-day sentence he originally handed her. As she was forcibly escorted from the courtroom, Paris screamed: 'Mom, Mom, Mom! It's not right.' Shortly after this, Paris's mother was later seen pacing the hallways of the court building, telling reporters, 'I'm paralyzed right now.'

As the media went into frenzy, speculation started as to what – if anything – Paris's 'unspecified' medical condition was. A friend claimed that maybe claustrophobia was the answer. 'It's not surprising to me that she was melting down because she was cooped up in a tiny cell 23 hours a day. When I heard that, I knew that would happen,' the friend told E! Online. 'I know her well enough to know she must have been flipping out. That's what happens to her. She can't breathe, her heart races and she feels like she's going to pass out! I knew it would be bad for her.'

Whatever the case, she was returned to a detention centre in Los Angeles, where she was believed to have undergone medical and psychiatric tests. The results of those tests are secret but soon after they were finished, Paris announced that she would not be launching another appeal against the judge's ruling. 'Today I told my attorneys not to appeal the judge's decision,' she said through her legal team. 'While I greatly appreciate the Sheriff's concern for my health and welfare, after meeting with doctors I intend to serve my time as ordered by the judge.

'This is by far the hardest thing I have ever done. During the past several days, I have had a lot of time to reflect and have already learned a bitter, but important lesson from this experience. As I have said before, I hope others will learn from my mistake. I have also had time to read the mail from my fans. I very much appreciate all of their good wishes and hope they will keep their letters coming.

'I must also say that I was shocked to see all of the

attention devoted to the amount of time I would spend in jail for what I had done by the media, public and city officials. I would hope going forward that the public and the media will focus on more important things, like the men and women serving our country in Iraq, Afghanistan and other places around the world.'

As we've seen, in the weeks leading up to Paris's court hearing, the media had tried to paint a picture of a young woman on a downward spiral. In reality, Paris had probably never been happier. Her friendship with Nicole Richie was back on track and her business ventures were, in the main, doing well. She also had a very special personal aspiration to fulfil. 'It's been my dream to have four babies by 30,' she said. 'I look after animals, so I'd have a lot to give my kids. I know in my heart of hearts I would be a great mother. I have a lot of beautiful animals that I look after and I feel that I would have a lot to give to my children. That's one important goal I want to achieve in my life and nothing has happened to change that. And I don't want to be an old mom – hopefully it'll happen soon, within the next five years. I would love to be as good a mother as my mother is to me. She is an amazing woman, a real inspiration to me.'

So Paris was, in fact, feeling positive and full of the excitement of life. 'I'm so happy. This is like a dream. You know, I'm so grateful to God that I have been blessed with all this, and I get to do what I love. I love my music, my acting, and I get to do everything I love. I just feel really excited, and I can't wait for the next day.

I'm excited to wake up every morning and just live my life.' She was loving the journey that is her life – and then came the prison sentence, like a huge 'Stop' sign, ready to throw all her positive feelings to one side and totally knock her off course.

As we've seen, just as Paris is idolised by millions, so is she envied by many. Beautiful, rich, happy and successful, she has long been the focal point of furious jealousy from those who feel they are none of those things. Therefore, in a strange way, Paris's jailing was a public service to such people who, as the media went into a frenzy over the story, had renewed opportunity to sneer at her.

This theory would, of course, have been little comfort to Paris as she sat in her jail cell. However, while the sentence was proving uncomfortable for Hilton the human being, for Hilton the celebrity it could prove to be little short of a godsend. She has often found that controversy can be the best way to keep herself in the public eye. When footage of her having sex with Rick Salomon was leaked onto the internet, she quickly turned it to her advantage. Paris could do the same with her jail term and use the sentence to propel her to even greater heights.

She was born not just with a silver spoon in her mouth, but also with a steely streak that means she can turn any setback to her advantage. Paris Hilton has probably already worked out how to use her jail term to lend her image a little more edge and keep her in the public eye for many years to come.

She'll be back stronger than ever – just you watch her.

FILMOGRAPHY

1991	*Wishman*
2000	*Sweetie Pie*
2002	*QIK2JDG*
	Nine Lives
2003	*The Cat In The Hat*
	Wonderland
	LA Knights
2004	*The Hillz*
	Raising Helen
2005	*Pledge This!*
	House Of Wax
2006	*Bottom's Up!*
2008	*The Hottie And The Nottie*

SELECTED BIBLIOGRAPHY

Hilton, Conrad N, *Be My Guest* (Prentice Hall, 1957)

Hilton, Paris, *Confessions Of An Heiress, A Tongue-in-Chic Peek Behind The Pose* (Fireside, 2004)

Hilton, Tinkerbell, *The Tinkerbell Hilton Diaries* (Warner Bros, 2004)

Mair, George, *Paris Hilton – The Naked Truth* (Chamberlain Bros, 2004)

Oppenheimer, Jerry, *House Of Hilton* (Crown, 2006)

Torres, Jennifer, *Paris Hilton* (Mitchell Lane, 2006)